THE LIMINAL

THE LIMINAL

NOTES ON LIFE, RACE AND DIRECT PROVISION

EDITED BY
FIADH MELINA

TALLAV

For those of us who live at the shoreline
standing upon the constant edges of decision
crucial and alone
for those of us who cannot indulge
the passing dreams of choice
who love in doorways coming and going
in the hours between dawns
looking inward and outward
at once before and after
seeking a now that can breed
futures
like bread in our children's mouths
so their dreams will not reflect
the death of ours

Audre Lorde
A Litany for Survival

"This place is a jungle"

Contents

i

THE NOTES

Profits from this anthology will go towards **The Danú Project**.

The Danú Project is a volunteer-run organisation, which provides day-to-day supports for people living in the Direct Provision system.

All funds will be dispersed between the three project branches: Maternity Kits, Mental Health Scheme, and Youth Outreach.

People seeking asylum are included in the decision making processes of projects to ensure the supports are relevant to actual needs.

For more information on The Danú Project:

www.danuproject.com

@thedanuproject

INTRODUCTION

DEDICATION

This book is important because it showcases issues that are not known by many. It is an opportunity for asylum seekers to express their pain, worry and fears. It's an appeal to the Irish public to act by pushing the government to treat people in Direct Provision better.

This book is for the asylum seekers in Direct Provision.

My life has taught me never to give up. Pain is a feeling that hurts but will heal. All problems have a solution. If no one sees your focus then make them see it. Fight for what is right and do it well.

Above all, love and forgive always; it sets you free.

Leefary 2021

A BOOK OF FEW ANSWERS

Fiadh Melina

Today, as I write this, a man in Cork thinks he might die in the next day or two. He is on hunger strike and has been for a week. Nadim Hussain lives in Direct Provision and is seeking asylum here in Ireland after anti-Muslim riots in West Bengal took the lives of his parents and threatened his own. "He fears he would be killed if he was to be deported to India" (Lee, 2021). Hussain began his strike after receiving the news that his application for international protection had been refused. The International Protection Appeal Tribunal (IPAT) decided Hussain would not receive refugee or subsidiary protection status and would face deportation. Hussain's strike is a plea to remain, and it is a reminder that Ireland's histories of hunger strikes and institutions are not in the past, but remain steadfast in the present.

This book will not provide you with all the answers, in fact it might not give you any. There isn't one solitary book that will unpack and dismantle our society, and still fit comfortably in your day-bag for a stroll to the park. You might find the book with all the answers in a university library, but it's probably in the short-loan section and is too large and bothersome to bring past the front doors. This is not that book.

This is the book I hope you will tear through in one (albeit long) sitting; the book you will dip in and out of when the need strikes; the book that will make you reassess yourself, your social circles and your country; the book that will make you ask how can I better the environment around me and what can I do next? Without looking at ourselves, we can't make the little and large changes needed to challenge a malfunctioning society. But what is a functioning society in reality? I'm not sure anyone has figured it out yet. In fact, in the ten thousand years of recorded civilised society began, it seems no one has quite put it into lasting practice. Perhaps one of you reading this will, which brings me back to what this book is. It is a book of questions (many of which are answerless and lead to more questions), a little starter guide to questioning you and your world and how it treats others. My toddler seems to have a better grasp on this than most adults, so maybe the first question is to ask why many of us lose our childhood wonder.

When I prompt self-reflection, I also hope some tangible, informed action will follow. The pages in this book should help with the informed portion of that. The tangibility is up to you. I recently recorded a panel event for this book where I said, 'Do the thing, don't just think about it.' So I'll repeat myself: Do the thing.

This is not to say you, the individual, are expected to change the world. In fact, you, the individual, must decentralise yourself from being a world-changing saviour. In her essay White Delusion, Marcia Gunn challenges the assumptions white people make when their activism is laced with ego and ignorance. In cases where you are an ally to a cause that does not directly affect you, remember, it is not about you. Misplaced empathy can easily turn into hijacking. Your allyship is valued, your activism helps, but remember, it is not about you. It is about the Other.

Edward Said was a Palestinian-American academic who helped paint the landscape of postcolonial studies, particularly through his 1978 book *Orientalism*, where he conceptualised the reception of the Other. Othering, in short, creates the dynamic of 'Us versus Them.' You will read a good deal about him and this theory in Sandrine Ndahiro's essay *Other*, as she uses Otherisation and contextualises it against the Direct Provision system. Said's legacy of postcolonial thought can be felt in many of the following pieces. Hopefully, they will help in decolonising an education system that has traditionally followed the status quo. Decolonising education is a breakthrough concept in university teaching, which attempts to reframe how history is taught and what histories are told. Carr and Lipscomb, in their 2021 anthology *What is History, Now?* define the decolonisation of curriculums as "considering the histories of race, empire and slavery...and attending to 'historical' experiences beyond those of the (usually) white colonisers. It is about diversifying the voices included in history rather than censoring them."

Othering, as a theoretical concept, entered my radar during my Classical studies at university. Classics sounds quite bougie, and the fact is, it has been, by the way it has been taught and who it has been taught to and by for centuries. But it is shifting. By its nature, Classics, the studies of Ancient Greece and Rome, is founded on the bedrock of colonialism and patriarchal systems. It is perhaps what fascinates me about it so much. I became transfixed by the cyclical and repetitive nature of human behaviour, by the repetitive rise and fall of empires, by what it is that unites peoples, and what drives people against other people, to conquer, expand, kill. This one, I do have a partial (simplified) answer for, and it is fear. Fear (usually unfounded) of the unknown, the different, the Other.

We Other automatically as a survival tactic. All of us do so subconsciously, it's inherent in the human experience. It is why Neanderthals no longer exist and we are all descended from Homo Sapiens, despite both species overlapping for a few hundred thousand years. Homo Sapiens, which evolved on the African continent, only fully populated the previously Neanderthal land of what is now Europe and much of Asia after the Neanderthal was wiped out through conflict.

Othering in Ireland takes many shapes. As the daughter of an immigrant mother in a rural Irish town, xenophobia was a thriving undercurrent. It still is. This is something many white immigrants or people of mixed white ethnicities will be familiar with. We are white, but not quite 'Irish white' enough to escape Othering in what was a starkly homogenous Ireland. The casual but derogatory notion of "the foreigners have come to take our jobs" is still entrenched in contemporary culture. Migrants are often (inaccurately) seen as threats to the native status quo. Particularly throughout adolescence I heard plenty of, 'Go back to X (all of which were inaccurate locations)' and 'How do I say (insert difficult surname)', and so on, but I do not suffer from systemic racism. This is where we, the white Irish, seem to misunderstand racial oppression. Later on, you will read and learn about these differences in my segment *Xenophobia or Racism: Which is it?* and Eric Ehigie's *The Problem with our National Conversation about Racism*.

Today, we frown upon the existence of Magdalene Laundries and Mother and Baby Homes, but have sat idly by as a new institution was formed only four years after the last Laundry was shut. Only this time the institution caters to a different group of people, a people that are easier to Other in our current society, therefore easier to view as lesser than. Othering, where modern concepts of race is involved, has developed into a derogatory rhetoric. It segregates based on skin colour which is a far easier identifier at-a-glance than, for example, class. It has created the view of Black and Indigenous peoples as subhuman or in fact, not human at all.

This is prevalent in medical racism, where Black, Brown, Asian and Indigenous people are still mistreated during pregnancy. For example, centuries-old theories about Black and Indigenous women having higher pain thresholds have caused the unnecessary withholding of epidurals or other forms of negligence based on subconscious racial and ethnic biases (Glaser, 2021). These theories are now absolutely debunked and stem from the racist idea that some communities are more animalistic and therefore require less medical intervention. Eliane Glaser's *Motherhood: A Manifesto* is based on the UK healthcare model, but it is a worldwide experience. In March 2020, Nayyab Tariq, a Brown-skinned woman died after giving birth to a healthy baby, because the staff could not discern what 'pale' looked like on darker skin and other signs of her worsening state were ignored. The HSE review stated, "One of the indications of a patient being in shock is when they appear pale [...] Skin pallor was initially less obvious due to ethnicity."

This book will use the terms black people, white people or BIPOC people because we live in a racialised society and this is easily digestible language. They are helpful now, to differentiate experiences, but unhelpful in that they don't take into account classism, ableism and a whole spectrum of nuanced experiences people from different corners of society live.

We like to categorise because we are human. It helps lessen the fear and creates order in a chaotic world. In school we learn a square is a square which is different from a rectangle, and sometimes there's a blue square and a red square but they're still both squares and their value is equal. Then come the bigger squares and little squares but that starts going into mathematical territory and I am not a mathematician so I will stop my shape analogies there. What I mean to say is, in school, we are taught not to think outside the box (or the square, hah). We are taught to learn the mould of categories and order.

As you read these terms which segregate by the colour of skin, keep in mind the difference in life experience varies as much within each 'category' as the categories vary between one another.

Have you ever questioned the use of terms such as 'the developing world', 'Third World countries', the Near East? Why not say southwestern Asia, as the land geographically stands? Do you understand that 'developing' and 'third-world' countries are those which have been exploited by colonial powers? Decolonising universities will challenge the status quo of colonial learning, however we should begin critical thinking before third-level education; it is an essential life lesson and should not be something only those who attend university can develop. Of course, I'm speaking of the Irish context. Public secondary-level education in Ireland did not teach me critical thinking, instead it has taught me that we leave fourteen years of education without learning how to think for ourselves, without thinking beyond a certain mould. In fact, when you do try to reach beyond the mould, you are often punished by mediocre grades.

We are a nation of shame but a people of guilt and both need to change. First, we need to understand the difference between shame and guilt, then we need to let go of both. This is not to say you should never feel guilt; guilt is an emotion with a vital, industrial quality to it that if inspected correctly can motivate change. Guilt as a sedentary thing is unhelpful.

Systemically, Ireland has hushed voices of the vulnerable and we look back, baffled by the crimes of the 'past', to which whisper our grievances. We'll say (still in a hushed tone), "Never again". But it happens again. Again. Again. Again.

Audre Lorde said, "Guilt is not a response to anger; it is a response to one's own actions or lack of action. If it leads to change then it can be useful, since it is then no longer guilt but the beginning of knowledge. Yet all too often, guilt is just another name for impotence, for defensiveness destructive of communication; it becomes a device to protect ignorance and the continuation of things the way they are, the ultimate protection for changelessness."

You may feel guilt for the several Aramark-owned Avoca scones you've consumed in the past, but as Emma Dabiri writes in *What White People Can Do Next*, "guilt is counterproductive." I use a light-hearted scone reference because it's maybe more digestible than accepting the alternatives, or maybe it's to spare triggering guilt in you, the reader, by using a more explicit analogy. Dabiri continues, "We cannot allow guilt and shame about acknowledging the past to paralyse us in a state of inaction and avoidance."

Though it may not give you many straightforward answers, I hope this anthology will leave you reaching for more, that it will give you a foundation to build from so you don't feel you are wading through the dark.

The Liminal doesn't tell all the stories, but each writer has had the opportunity to recommend further reading, podcasts or other media which can help you continue learning and engaging. I urge you to follow up on these.

We have only scratched the surface here. There is space for commentary on ableism, colourism and queer experiences within Direct Provision and the Irish activist community. The story of Sylva Tukula is one of many queer stories of state negligence. A transwoman housed in an all-male Direct Provision centre in Galway, Sylva's identity wasn't respected by the state in life. Nor was she respected by the state in death. After she passed in 2018, Sylva was buried without any of her friends present; the state did not alert anyone of the details and couldn't attend. The state had stopped releasing details of deaths in Direct Provision in 2017.

As I finish writing this, Nadim Hussain has ended his hunger strike on its ninth day. The Department of Justice assured Hussain he will not be deported. The doctors informed Hussain he has pancreatitis as a result of his fast. The mental traumas are

I hope, from this singular story and the others throughout the anthology, you reading this will understand the system does not work. A functioning system would not force more trauma upon anyone seeking protection. It is the dysfunction of the Direct Provision system that we will unfold in this book, and the broader dysfunctional systems in our society which have allowed it to exist.

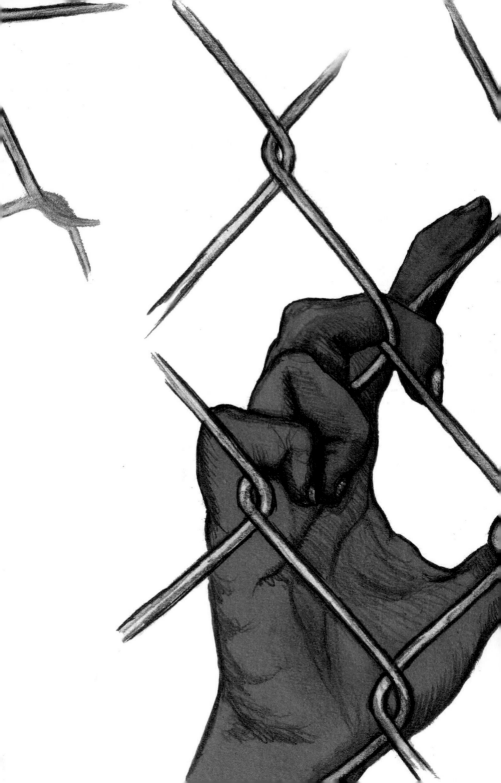

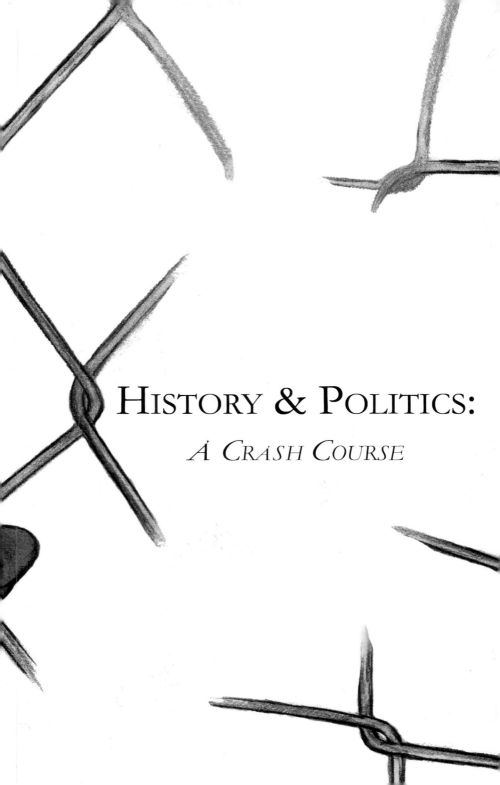

HISTORY & POLITICS:

A CRASH COURSE

Uaigneas an Chladaigh: We Owe it to the Past

In Thirty-Two Words for Field, an expansive journey through Irish vocabulary and its connection to our landscape, the author Manchán Magan captured a phrase quite relevant to the generational, migratory spirit of the Irish. Uaigneas an chladaigh quite literally translates to 'loneliness of the shore,' but Irish has a musicality about it which often gets lost in direct translation. What uaigneas an chladaigh means is, 'the feeling there are ancestral spirits on the shore'.

Ireland is a land of island culture, assigned so by geography. The country's historical, economic, political and social landscape has been shaped by the coast. Before fully getting into the present, it is important to note the past and the role it has played in creating the situation of today. We often look at our more recent history in order to categorise what being Irish means, but this is a shortsighted view which only dulls the true vitality of Irish identity.

Before Irish Independence, before Ireland was a British colony, there came a thousand years of shifting culture. Pre-Celtic Ireland became Celtic Ireland, the Vikings came, and so too did Normans and French Huguenots. The influences of all of these cultures run in our present. Why then, has Irish identity come with a prologue of exclusion rather than inclusion?

It can likely be blamed on the need to create an exclusive Irish identity in post-Independence Ireland, an identity that differed the newly independent population from its colonisers. Unfortunately, as happens when there is a sudden vacuum in power structures, something enters to fill the void. In Ireland's case, this was Catholicism, which allowed its people to create an identity which diverged from the predominantly Protestant British. The nature of the Catholic Church however, also brought with it a surge of conservatism throughout the nineteenth century, the repercussions of which we still experience today. Strict laws banning divorce, abortion and contraception are examples of this which were only amended in the last forty years. Acknowledgement of the melting-pot Ireland that came before the British and the Catholic Church was largely snuffed out.

Ireland has migration ingrained in her sociocultural history, which makes it impossible to answer the question, "What is Irishness?" If we take a deep look at our history, we'll actually find ourselves on the barbaric side, as the Other, more often than not.

Celtic Ireland was the land of druids and pagan religion. The Romans called the Celts barbarians and largely wiped them out during their imperial expansion across Europe in the first centuries CE. The Irish under British rule were also barbarised, seen as lesser than, which left us with the situation which is commonly called the Famine, however genocide is more accurate. There was a blight that affected the potato crops during the Great Hunger of nineteenth century Ireland, but there was still enough food to cater to the eight million people who lived on the land. Despite this, the British continued exports of grains which could have saved the lives of one million Irish people. Another million were forced to emigrate. We look at this emigration almost lightheartedly today, as something positive, because we must. The Irish have roots everywhere, it seems. This is great.

"Irishness is not simply territorial," Mary Robinson said in her 1995 speech Cherishing the Irish Diaspora. If this claim was made twenty-six years ago, it shouldn't be much of a surprise today. Time, after all, makes broad concepts more digestible. However, the support of the broader Irish public behind this statement is feeble at best even though we are now in 2021, a far more liberal Ireland than the one of 1995.

The 'protect our own' sentiment surges in times of mass immigration or heightened homelessness, when there is sudden outcry of "But we have 10,000 homeless, help them first!". It is generally the people who do not partake in any social activism who make statements like this, and therefore do not understand it is not a case of 'us' versus 'them.' There are are currently 58 'ghost estates' across Ireland and at least a thousand more partially built homes which could, if followed through with proper governmental action, help the housing crisis (O'Doherty, 2021). "Help our own!" or "Help the homeless," are empty statements which only segregate those in need of shelter and do not provide protection to either. Safe shelter is a human right and Ireland is failing to provide this on many counts. This does not mean pitting those seeking shelter against one another, it means creating collective action to house all. 'Protect our own,' is racist, and it generally only encompasses a select type of person who looks a certain way, in this case, white. But Irish identity is still young and ever-changing, it is not too late to counteract the establishment of institutionalised racism the way it has been rooted in the likes of the United States, France and Britain. "The concept of whiteness may be well established [here in Ireland], but the institutionalised intergenerational racism hasn't had the same opportunities to take root. Before it does, it's time to create new stories."

Over seventy million people worldwide can claim Irish descent with pride, this should translate to a tolerance for diversity which is not running with undercurrents and often blatant xenophobia and racism. Robinson said, "Our relation with the diaspora beyond our shores is one which can instruct our society in the values of diversity, tolerance, and fair-mindedness." It still stands today as it did in 1995. The relationship we have with the diaspora beyond our shores should remind us that identity is as fluid as the sea our people have crossed time and time again. It should remind us that being Irish is more than living on this island or having a certain skin colour or religious belief.

Xenophobia or Racism: Which is it?

There are many *phobias* and *isms* circulating in culture today. There are equally as many *ists* who belong to the isms, and bigots who belong to both. That may seem like a foreign language, and in some ways, if you are not constantly engaged with the sociopolitical landscape, it is.

The language we use today has grown to suit new thoughts and ideas, postcolonialisms and intersectional feminisms and everything else that lies in the sociopolitical spectrum. Language has morphed to suit social media and the fast-paced information consumption that goes along with it. There is so much information all the time that at some point it becomes too much, and we hit barriers like misinformation and outrage fatigue. With so much information constantly circulating, it can be difficult to fact check and comprehend what is truth and what is semi-truth or not truth at all. With so much information of horrors and the tribulations of society, it can be difficult to remain constantly engaged, in fact, it is impossible without eventual burnout.

Within this sphere of morphed language are two words which are not new, but have come to mean certain things and are sometimes mixed up. In the Irish context, racism and xenophobia are often used interchangeably and incorrectly. There is a misconception that, because the white Irish have suffered under colonialism and were forced into servitude in the Caribbean alongside black slaves, that we too have suffered racism. This is not the case.

The Irish were contracted into indentured servitude, which could be worked off after a number of years and any children born to indentured servants were not automatically labelled the same. This was different to the black slaves who could not work to gain freedom and whose children were automatically born into slavery. The Irish were sent across the Atlantic as second-class citizens due to xenophobia, due to the British view that the Irish were lesser than. The systemic racism black people and other people of colour have faced worldwide is not comparable to the xenophobic experience of the white Irish. Though the Irish faced severe xenophobia at the hands of the British and were considered barbaric to a degree, they were still white and able to embrace whiteness and the privileges that come along with it.

Xenophobia comes from the Greek roots *xenos*, and *phobos*; the latter is commonly known to mean fear. In its most simple translation, xenos means foreigner or stranger. However, as explained by Cambridge classicist Anne Thompson, it can also mean an ally, a lifelong friend, a guest, and a host. The negative connotations depend on the culture adapting its use but in modern culture its negative connotations are far more common. Xenophobia literally means 'fear of a foreigner' or 'fear of someone from someplace else' or 'fear of a stranger.'

However it is important to clarify that a xenophobe is not someone who is fearful of foreigners by any realistic threat, rather a xenophobe holds prejudiced sentiments towards foreigners which creates hatred and is expressed through discrimination. Intolerance and discrimination can be expressed through varying degrees of intensity. It includes, derogatory statements like, "They will take our jobs!"; microaggressive name mispronunciation; supporting political figures who run anti-immigration campaigns; violence against someone due to their origin. The list goes on. Xenophobic statements, whether 'big' or perceptibly 'small' are all harmful.

The use of phobos (fear) itself subconsciously alters the perception of the word and has allowed xenophobes (and all other phobes) to shift victim status onto themselves.

Racism has grown out of modern concepts of what race is. "Race is one of the most powerful, seductive and enduring myths of the last four centuries. [...] The concept of a white race and a black race is not something that exists in nature (Dabiri, 2021)." Certainly, there was no concept of race in terms of black and white two thousand years ago, where the word xenos was originally used. The classical empires who coined the term called everyone barbarian, Othered everyone who spoke different languages or practiced different ways of life; they were explicitly xenophobic (very typical of colonialists), but not racist, because racism as we know it, did not exist. What we now consider racial difference (the colour of a person"s skin) was only first codified into law in 1661.

Creating a system of race was a strategic play in order to fabricate the illusion of superior (white) and inferior (black) races. It allowed the purging of the African continent and upheld slavery and segregation in what later became the United States. The first slave ship landed in what is now Virginia in 1619, the Thirteenth Amendment was passed to abolish slavery in 1865, and racial segregation ended with the passing of the Civil Rights Act of 1964.

The legacy of racism exists today because it is part of modern history. It exists worldwide and still disproportionately affects black, indigenous and people of colour because infrastructure of those groups were upheaved by colonial powers led by white supremacy. The rebuilding of said infrastructure has often been thwarted by the continued physical or psychological presence of colonial powers. Racism as it exists today is unique to each country and that country's relationship to colonialism, homogeny and many other variables. This is why it is not yet too late to stop Ireland from falling into the toxic, systemically racist patterns of other countries.

It is, of course, possible to be both racist and xenophobic. Nearly all racism is laced with xenophobia. "Where are you from?" or "Where are you really from?" or "Where are your parents from originally?" are examples of this. While in Ireland it is common to ask where anyone is from out of the cosy notion that everyone knows someone who knows someone from X, Y, Z county, there is a certain way these questions are framed when someone has been Othered.

In Ireland, these questions will be posed to someone with skin that is not white, or to someone who is white but has a different accent, because their belonging is easier to question. These are very simple examples and there are many complexities and combinations of Othering that people use consciously or subconsciously to project xenophobia and/or racism.

Systems of oppression often work in favour of one another. We can view this in *misogynoir*; a unique experience black women face at the intersection of being both subject to misogyny and racist systems; within this there can be homophobic systems which discriminate against people. We can view this in the traveling community in Ireland, where classism and xenophobia collide; within this there can be ableist systems further discriminating people. There are sub-communities within every community which is why intersectionality is an important concept to become acquainted with.

HOSPITALITY PARADOX: *CÉAD MÍLE FÁILTE*

Ireland is famed as the Land of a Hundred Thousand Welcomes, a phrase which has become tiresome when used in reference to Direct Provision, but the irony is unignorable. There is welcome when there is economic gain; our tourism sector in 2019 (pre-pandemic) saw a combined oversees and domestic revenue of over €9bn (Fáilte Ireland, 2021).

Tourism in Ireland is vibrant and welcoming to all, whether the tourists are solo travelers staying in hostels and hiking mountains, couples on a city break, families heading to the coasts or an amalgamation of the lot. Old and young, and people of all backgrounds are greeted with smiles and banter.

As Ireland rose in various sectors on the world stage at the turn of the millennium, the rise in international protection applicants began to overwhelm the existing system. The state acts very differently towards those seeking asylum than it does to those bringing disposable income. This lacks a sense of longevity because there are of course many highly skilled and entrepreneurial people living in Direct Provision who could aid growth in economy through long-term support programs.

Programs like this could prepare international protection applicants for the hiring processes in Ireland, upgrade English proficiency levels where needed and ensure there is a conversion system in place for international qualifications. Alongside creating a stable workforce that is ready for integration, this would help ease the limbo-like nature of life in Direct Provision. Many people living in the system have no structure to their days aside from set meal times. Courses and active participation towards integration would aid in creating much needed daily stability during the asylum process.

In 1999, the Irish government replaced the system in place for housing and processing people seeking asylum and created a new system called Direct Provision. Direct Provision was designed to temporarily house and process international protection applicants for a maximum of six months. It was introduced due to the sudden surge in asylum seeking applicants arriving. From early 2000 onwards, people were processed through the new system, but the reception and accommodation centres were also insufficient to deal with the new numbers of protection applicants in a timely and humane manner. For reference, in 1996 there were 1,179 applications for international protection; in 2000, 2001 and 2002 there were 10,938, 10,325 and 11,634 respectively.

Previously, people seeking asylum could apply for social welfare but were not allowed to seek work. The ease of access to the social welfare system in the late nineties created discontent among 74% of Irish people (Hilliard, 2019). Public as much as governmental upheaval was the cause for the establishment of Direct Provision. Four years earlier, in October 1996, Ireland closed the doors to its final

Magdalene Laundry, much to the public's relief. With it, the two-centuries long era of institutionalised living for vulnerable people in Ireland had come to a close, or so it seemed. With the opening of Direct Provision, the Irish State returned to a familiar method of dealing with people it rathered have hidden away.

The strain on Direct Provision was caused by inadequate infrastructure or forward thinking. In order to cater to the high numbers still arriving in the early 2000s, the government resorted to hiring private contractors to provide catering services in centres where there were no cooking facilities, and private-run centres began to crop up.

In 2021, there are seven state-owned Direct Provision centres, and thirty-eight private-owned or 'commercial' centres (IPAS, 2021). These commercial centres cost the government a fortune to keep open. They are hotels, guesthouses and other buildings which are often not fit for purpose. The companies hired to provide catering to centres have repeatedly been reported to violate humane standards of provisions. Many concerns have been raised by people living in the system regarding their health as a direct result from unhealthy food. The limited choice available in catering accommodations are a caused by severe culture-blindness. For example, people have requested whether the meats are prepared through halal methods and were told that it was, only to later find out that they had been lied to. Meal times are also at set times which can be problematic for those fasting for Ramadan.

Perhaps the greatest failure of Direct Provision is the time spent by people in the system. Despite being designed as a short-term accommodation solution, the reality is that some people have lived in Direct Provision for over a dozen years. One woman has lived in

Direct Provision for seventeen years. Pamela Uba, who became the first black woman to win Miss Ireland, lived in a centre for ten years throughout her childhood. The current average time for people living in the system is two years. The system was designed to house people for six months, not ten years, and certainly not seventeen.

In February 2021, the Irish Government released the White Paper which outlined a plan to change the current system of Direct Provision and replace it with a more humane system by 2024. In theory, the ambitious new system will improve integration and the basic rights of those seeking international protection. The "new approach will end congregated and institutional living. Instead it focuses on supporting integration from day one. Applicants will initially reside in a Reception and Integration Centre, with own-door or own-room accommodation, where they will be assigned a case-worker and receive wrap-around supports, healthcare and education. Within a short period of time, this support will extend to include access to housing and employment in order to prepare them, and enable them, to live independently within the community." (O'Gormon, 2021).

The White Paper plan, though a welcome step towards ending Direct Provision, has many shortcomings and is already behind schedule. These shortfalls are outlined by the Movement of Asylum Seekers in Ireland (MASI) in a statement released on February 26th in response to the White Paper's release. Primary concerns included the fact that "none of these changes will be implemented through legislation," which puts at risk the validity of the four-month assigned housing limit. "This is problematic as people might end up in the system longer with no way of holding the state to account if it happens, as it has been the case with Direct Provision." MASI was also concerned by the lack of support offered to those seeking asylum if they did not first spend four months in the system.

The realities of own-room accommodation being provided for single people were also a concern. Own-room accommodation would solve the issue of strangers sharing rooms and overcrowding, however it would be possible only by student-style co-living spaces, where living room, kitchen and other areas are communal. While there is scope here for community building within apartments/communal spaces, it still forces strangers into sharing spaces under stressful conditions. If disputes were to arise (likely, according to MASI), there would need to be a clear legislature or rule process in place in order to settle such disputes.

The right to work would remain restricted until months after an application for asylum has been submitted. This halts integration and stagnates the lives of those able to work from day one. In the meantime, both MASI and the Irish Refugee Council have strongly recommended that the weekly Daily Expenses Allowance provided to asylum seekers be made higher in order to decrease poverty rates within the system.

MIGRANT, REFUGEE OR ASYLUM SEEKER: WHICH IS IT?

The media portrays immigration in a uniform way which usually means you will see an image of a boat on the Mediterranean Sea, filled with brown or black people, with a voiceover using the term 'migrants'. It is true most people living in Direct Provision centres are from BIPOC communities. It is true 'migrant' encompasses the general experience of those moving from one country to another, but there are social connotations that lie with the word migrant which are harmful to the experience of those fleeing violence and persecution.

The Cambridge Dictionary defines a migrant as 'a person that travels to a different country, often to find work.' The inclusion of often to find work points towards an economic migrant, which is what instantly triggers anti-immigration rhetoric. Further complicating things, the dictionary's example of the word in a sentence is; The cities are full of migrants looking for work. Miriam-Webster gives an even more outdated definition and defines a migrant as 'a person who moves regularly in order to find work especially in harvesting crops.' The example given is 'migrants in search of work on farms.'

This collectivity becomes unhelpful when we would like to

differentiate between the types of people migrating and understand that not all who arrive on our shores (whether this be by boat or plane or otherwise) arrive on equal footing. Not everyone arrives with the same rights, because not everyone's journey was the same, because not everyone's reasons for migrating were the same, because everyone has their unique story.

At this point, you might be wondering why being so focused upon a small definition is taking up so much space. The reason is, language matters. It always has, because we are creatures of language and subconsciously or consciously put meaning to the language we consume.

People leave their home countries for various reasons, some of which are to find a more economically sustainable place of living, without fear of persecution driving them. Many however are not economically-led, and this is where the term migrant (as the dictionaries define it) fails. The use of migrant, and the subconscious attachments we have with the word, is a strategic one which is harmful to those seeking asylum. It is a tactic which can be used to question the legitimacy of a person's claim for protection.

When people flee persecution and/or human rights violations in their home countries they are eligible to seek international protection. Reasons for forced displacement can include but are not limited to; war and violence; threats linked to climate crises; poverty; threats due to sexuality, gender and religion.

When international protection applicants reach foreign borders, they are subject to that specific country's processes. In Ireland's case, they are housed in Direct Provision while their applications are under review. They might also stay in Direct Provision after they have received refugee status, until a suitable place of living has been found. In Ireland's rental market, this can take months. If a person has already been through a refugee camp and granted refugee status before entering, they are processed in a different way.

Asylum Seeker: A person seeking international protection as a refugee, but has not yet received refugee status by the governing authorities of the country from which they seek protection. In Ireland, people seeking asylum are boarded in Direct Provision centres, often indefinitely, until their applications are processed. This may take weeks or years, and an asylum seeker may face deportation if their application is unsuccessful. This decision can be appealed by the applicant.

Refugee: A person who has been granted refugee status. There are different types of refugees. Some begin their claims as asylum seekers in ireland; some (program refugees) have their claims evaluated in refugee camps abroad, and once granted refugee status, are taken in by countries who have signed up to provide protection.

As designated by the 1951 RC, refugees deserve, as a minimum, the same standards of treatment enjoyed by other foreign nationals in a given country and, in many cases, the same treatment as nationals. In Ireland, refugees are entitled to remain indefinitely. They can apply for family reunification and Irish citizenship after 3 years. There are refugee grants in place for students wishing to pursue third level education. Refugees can't return to the country they're seeking protection from for

5 years.

Subsidiary Protection: If it is decided that a person is not a refugee, they may qualify for subsidiary protection if there are substantial grounds for believing they would face a real risk of suffering serious harm if returned to their country of origin/country of former habitual residence. This is a status which is similar to that of refugee.

It is granted where the person does not qualify as a refugee but where the IPO considers that the person faces a real risk of suffering serious harm in his or her country of origin. People with subsidiary protection are given many of the same rights as an Irish citizen.

Rights of International Protection Applicants (Asylum Seekers) in Ireland

Each person seeking asylum gets a Daily Expenses Allowance. The weekly rate in 2021 is €29.80 for a child and €38.80 for adults. This is expected to cover menstrual and hygiene products, food, travel expenses, clothes and other supplies. The Daily Expenses Allowance was originally introduced in 2000, with a rate of IR£15 (€19.10) per adult and IR£7.50 (€9.60) per child. The low rate however, was impossible for people to live on, and after much campaigning by groups within the Direct Provision system, the rate was raised to €21.60 for each adult and child.

The Daily Expenses Allowance is still too low to sustain most day-to-day life. €38.80 per week breaks down to approximately €5.50 per day. There is the added problem of many Direct Provision centres being located in remote locations, so where there are private, on-site grocery shops available, the prices are often heightened. There are cases reported by residents where managers change the prices on a whim, for example the price of a block of cheese or bag of carrots one could vary from week to week, making it impossible to budget. Not every centre provides catering, therefore budgeting for meals is essential for those who have cooking facilities.

Many mothers in Direct Provision choose to feed by formula or need to for various reasons. In fact, breastfeeding health is highly affected by a pregnancy's environment. If this is the route she had planned, the stressors of Direct Provision can negatively affect the prospects of a mother's breastfeeding journey. This means the nutritional development of her child will be dependent on formula. Many centres do not provide infant formula or any other infant products to their residents. According to UNICEF, the average cost for powdered formula in the UK ranges from £6.44 to £13.52 (c. €7.62 to €16.00). Before formula costs, there is the purchase of bottles, sterilisers, bottle brushes and varied teat sizes to contend with. Though there is an Exceptional Needs Payment which can be availed of, this usually ranges from €50-100 and is expected to also cover a pram, sling and other maternity essentials. In short, raising a child in Direct Provision has often led to a parent deciding to go hungry in order to feed their child.

Children under 16 must attend primary and post-primary education, which are free to attend. There is a Back to School Clothing and Footwear Allowance available to parents who have children starting or returning to school in September, it is also available to people aged 18-22 who may be returning to second-level education.

Access to the Allowance depends on the amount of kids attending, whether the parent has the right to work and receives a certain income, and other variables. There are no grants in place to aid in third level education.

Since July 2018, asylum seekers can apply for permission to work in Ireland under certain criteria. The right to work still has many limitations and remains a major hurdle in the rights available to asylum seekers in ireland. A person can apply for a work permit six months after applying for asylum in Ireland and if they are not granted the right to work, this decision can be appealed. The appeal process can take months, and there is no guarantee of a positive result. In early 2021, an asylum seeker went on hunger strike after their right to work had been denied. The person needed to earn in order to send money to their parents who remained in Syria and could not support themselves. The person did not have the option of returning to Syria, having fled torture.

Even where a person does receive a permit to work, there are many logistical and social barriers which hinder them from entering employment such as:

- Discrimination based on ethnicity, race, religion,
- Psychological distress caused by the asylum process,
- Rural locations of Direct Provision centres are often far from employment opportunities,
- Language,
- Access to (affordable) childcare,
- Lack of references,
- Limited or no recognition of existing qualifications,
- Doubt over the validity of work permits issued by the state. This has been an increasingly frequent complaint by asylum seekers who attempt to enter the workplace, only for their permit papers to be rejected by employers. This is caused by 'unofficial looking' documents which employers (wrongly) believe are forged by the jobseeker.

Asylum seekers are expected to stay at their assigned regional centre while their application for international protection (refugee status or subsidiary protection) is being processed. They are not allowed to seek alternative accommodation in the private rental sector during this time. Absenteeism from the designated accommodation centre for more than 3 consecutive nights can result in the reception and integration agency deeming their bed abandoned. Continuous absenteeism (3+ nights) will be taken as an indication that an asylum seeker does not wish to receive any aid or assistance from the agency.

House rules are posted in each accommodation centre at the discretion of the centre manager. As a resident in the centre, an asylum seeker is expected to abide by these rules. Complaints regarding rules must first be made to the centre manager. If it is unresolved it can be put to the IPAS, and beyond that, to the Ombudsman. However, the complaint process can often be inaccessible, as an asylum seeker's application may be threatened if they submit complaints. Managers have been known to make a resident's life more difficult if they are found to submit a complaint.

Hunger Strikes, Life and Death in Ireland

Between 2017 and 2021, the Department of Children, Equality, Disability, Integration and Youth stopped releasing the figures of those who died in the Direct Provision system. This secrecy ended in February 2021 after public and intergovernmental pressure. Between 2007 and 2017, forty-four people died in Direct Provision, including three stillborn babies and one neonatal death, according to information released under Freedom Of Information (FOI). In 2020, due to the mishandling of the COVID-19 outbreak in overcrowded Direct Provision Centres, fourteen individuals died of COVID-19.

Over the years, many people have developed cholesterol and heart issues due to the high-fat foods served by catering companies in some centres. There was a report of a man dying by heart failure in a canteen in front of other residents which traumatised the children. The resident who reported this claims it was due to the food provided. It is impossible to give an accurate number of deaths that have happened in Direct Provision due to the lack of records between 2017 and 2021.

There is no centralised record of names, dates, nationalities or cause of death for people who have applied for International Protection in Ireland, and who die while living in Direct Provision centres.

Due to the numerous human rights violations committed since Direct Provision was founded, hunger strikes have taken place within accommodation centre walls. There have been hunger strikes prompted by major issues such as the right to work, leave to remain and the inadequate nutritional provisions within centres. All strikes have been for access to basic human rights. This continues a legacy of Irish protest by the oppressed against their oppressors.

Hunger strikes, as a form of protest, date back to the Brehon Laws of Early Medieval Ireland. Traditionally, the breaking of oral legal codes were fixed through a self-help system, so it was up to the individual to right any wrongs committed against them. Fasting at a wrongdoer's doorstep became a method of protest for the powerless against the powerful.

Due to the high value placed on hospitality at the time, it was taboo to allow someone to starve and die at their doorstep. Death rarely occurred as a result of these early hunger strikes, as the striker's demands were met before it could progress to that. Hunger striking is not unique to Ireland, but since pre-Christian times, it has frequently been resorted to in order to challenge the country's socio-political troubles.

Hunger strikes have heroic origins in our folklore too. In a political context, hunger strikes became a traditional form of protest by those backed into a corner with no other options; a weapon of last resort. The earliest strikes in the 20th century date back to the women's suffrage movement, where twenty-two Irish women protested during their imprisonment between 1912 and 1914. There were nationalist

Hunger strikes throughout the next decade; e.g. in protest of the 1921 Anglo Irish Treaty. Commonly, hunger strikes have been used in political protest to undermine British presence on the island of Ireland. Hunger strikes took place during the DeValera period of rule, and resurfaced in the 1970s during the Troubles.

Key Terms

International Protection Accommodation Services (IPAS): was formerly called the Reception and Integration Agency (RIA). IPAS is responsible for the provision of services to asylum seekers and refugees, coordinating the implementation of integration policy for all refugees and persons granted subsidiary status and leave to remain in the Republic of Ireland, and responding to crisis situations which may result in large numbers of refugees arriving in the country.

IPAS is responsible for providing residential accommodation and essential services to asylum seekers while they await the outcome of their applications for asylum in the country. The Accommodation Procurement Unit of the agency has contracted various private companies such as Aramark to provide these services at several accommodation centres. The system has been criticised by human rights organisations as illegal, inhumane and degrading.

The Department of Justice: is in charge of the advancement of community and national security, the promotion of justice and equality and safeguarding of human rights.

The Department runs under two pillars, Civil Justice and Criminal

Justice, each led by a Deputy Secretary General. Each pillar contains the following functions: Policy, Legislation, Governance, and Operations & Service Delivery.

The Secretary General is the senior civil servant and non-political head of the Department. Their job is day-to-day management and non-political strategic planning and direction. They are also the Accounting Officer, and are responsible for safeguarding the funds under the control of the Department and for ensuring economy and efficiency in the running of the Department.

The Minister for Justice has responsibility for immigration matters in Ireland through two organisations:

- The Immigration Service is an executive office of the Department of Justice. It is responsible for undertaking the administrative functions of the Minister for Justice in relation to immigration, visa, international protection and citizenship matters. www.irishimmigration.ie

- Garda National Immigration Bureau (GNIB) is an office of An Garda Síochána (the Irish Police force). The office is responsible for all Garda matters relating to immigration on a national basis, mainly border control, registrations, granting permission to remain, deportations and investigations relating to illegal immigration and human trafficking. www.garda.ie

More info on www.justice.ie

International Protection Office (IPO): functions within the Department of Justice and is responsible for examining and processing applications for international protection under the International Protection Act 2015.

The IPO is an office within the Immigration Service Delivery (ISD), and the Irish Naturalisation and Immigration Service (INIS). It also considers, as part of a single procedure process, whether applicants should be given permission to remain.

The IPO is led by a Chief International Protection Officer who heads a team of international protection officers. who are independent in the performance of their international protection functions.

More info on www.ipo.gov.ie

The Department of Children, Equality, Disability, Integration and Youth (DCEDIY): deals with policy and service developments relating to a number of very important groups in society. It seeks to coordinate and develop key actions across Government relating to children and young people.

The DCEDIY works on issues relating to some of Ireland's most vulnerable groups including children at risk, children in care of the state, and other vulnerable, minority and disadvantaged groups. It emphasises inclusivity and support in the area of equality. It is responsible for international protection accommodation for those seeking asylum in Ireland and, in the near future, it will take on responsibility for disability services that are currently under the remit of the Department of Health.

The Department also deals with a range of important legacy issues from Ireland's past (it controls data on governmental projects like the Mother and Baby Homes Commission of Investigation, and the

Magdalen Restorative Justice Ex-Gratia Scheme).

They also deal with issues such as early learning and care for children, prevention and early intervention services and support and advice for parents.

The DCEDIY is made up of five divisions:
- Child Policy and Tusla Governance Division;
- Early Learning and Care and School-Age Childcare Division;
- Corporate and Business Support Division;
- Youth Justice, Adoption, Youth and Participation Division;
- Justice, International Protection and Equality Division;
- Unaccompanied children and young people are accepted into Ireland under the care of Tusla, the Child and Family Agency and are referred into the care of the Social Work Team for Separated Children Seeking Asylum (SWTSCSA).

More info on www.gov.ie/en/organisation/department-of-children-equality-disability-integration-and-youth/

Irish Refugee Protection Programme (IRPP): was established in September 2015 within the Office for the Promotion of Migrant Integration (OPMI). OMPI functions under the Department of Justice.

The IRPP was created after the State agreed to accept 4,000 refugees in response to the upsurge in refugee numbers in Italy, Greece, Lebanon and Jordan. The programme works alongside the European Union's Relocation Programme and the UNHCR-led Refugee Resettlement Programme.

In August 2021, The Justice Department announced that Ireland had allocated 150 IRPP places to Afghans after the Taliban's takeover of Afghanistan. Many others still await other avenues of protection.

More info on www.integration.ie/en/isec/pages/irpp

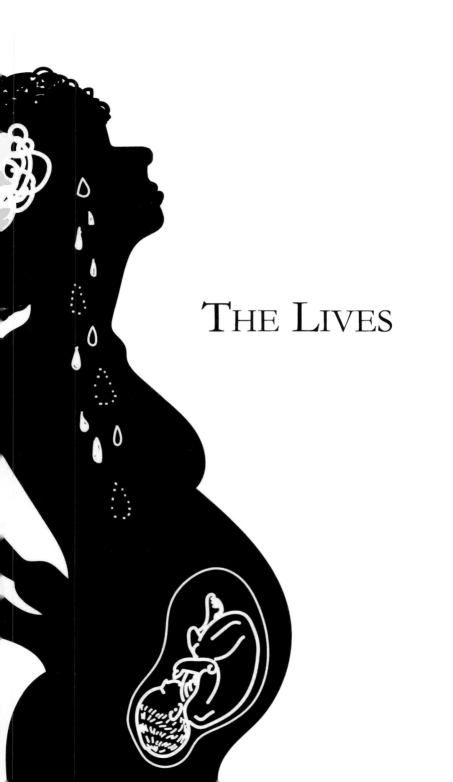

THE LIVES

A note on 'The Lives'

The Lives is a section of submissions by people
currently seeking asylum.

All submissions are anonymous.

Minimal editing has been done to each submission to
keep the original voice and tone of the individual.
Any revisions have been reviewed by the individual
and confirmed before printing.

I was like a dying flower but now I am alive again and blooming

I am a refugee woman. I finished university in my home country. I am an educated woman!

When I was very young, I was obligated by my family (as it was a common issue in our country) to get married with a man who was much older than me. There were so many differences between us. My husband couldn't make children, and I didn't have any problem. I am sure the problem was related to him, but he blamed me and said that I am infertile.

My life was very difficult. I was treated badly, the only way was to escape from this life and find a safe place. It wasn't accepted by the family and my husband, but I did because I had no other choice. I didn't want to leave my country and family, but life forced me to.

I had been through a hard time; I always wanted to solve the issues and have a simple and normal life, but nothing changed! It got worse day after day. I was about to lose my personality although I wanted to be a strong and courageous woman, but they wouldn't let me be. The doors were closed and I couldn't find a way to escape from the problems. I was like a bird in a cage. I wanted to find a place. Just a safe place, nothing more. I decided to escape with my boyfriend, and we came to Ireland.

When we arrived here, they sent me to a hotel. I was with 5 girls in one room for a short period of time. It was not a comfortable place and even the bathroom we shared was not safe. After that, they transferred us to another hotel. We stayed there for about one year. It was not a good place, the food was not healthy, and wasn't clean or safe!

us to another hotel. It was not a good place, the food was not healthy, and wasn't clean or safe!

Back then, Covid-19 pandemic started. They didn't follow the rules of protection, and the supervisor did not respect us and others, and didn't listen to us. A few days after we arrived at this hotel, I became sick. They took me to hospital and told me that I am pregnant. I was shocked and didn't believe it. I asked to do another test to make sure about it, because it had been many years that I hadn't become pregnant! I was shocked because it has been my dream for so long to become a mother but I was somehow sad due to not having a stable life here, and my own culture doesn't accept having a baby from a boyfriend. It is considered a sin.

After that, we went back to the hotel. It was sad. I was in a bad psychological condition as I was afraid to come out of the hotel and didn't want anyone to know that I am pregnant.

Being in that hotel with this unprofessional supervisor made my life much worse. Back then I had to visit a doctor to follow up my pregnancy weekly and monthly. That supervisor was not treating us like human beings. The supervisor sent me with 4 or 5 other people in one car who were not living in the same hotel and made the journey longer because picking them up and dropping them off took about 4.5 hours!

And it didn't follow any protection rules related to Covid-19. It was hard for me. I was afraid of getting infected and my condition because of my early pregnancy was hard, I had nausea and the hospital was very far. I couldn't breathe in the car. I didn't want to lose my baby!

If I asked the supervisor to send me with two people, not four, they said I could take a taxi by myself. Sometimes I didn't go to the hospital due to this reason. I did not have the money for it.

Even if I asked for something in the hotel they didn't answer. For example, I asked for a small refrigerator as we didn't have one in our room. They didn't answer us. I couldn't eat the food from the hotel for 9 months of my pregnancy. I had diabetes. I had to have healthy eating that was prescribed by the doctor.

Being pregnant and becoming a mother was a milestone for me as I had been waiting to achieve this dream for so long. I was about to deliver my baby during this hard time. Covid-19 made it harder for me as no one was allowed to be with me in the hospital. I was there for 3 days. I had labor, and it was very painful. It was between fear of dying or living! I can't forget!

After I delivered my baby (a natural birth), I was happy! It was a new chapter of my life, the nurses were very helpful and supportive. But still I couldn't sleep because I was worried about my baby.

Now, my baby is growing! She is an amazing baby! She is my happiness! I take care of her and can be a perfect parent for her. After several months they transferred us to a new place. A bigger one with lots of good people around us. I can have more fun and cook for us!

I want to nurture my child in a way that she will have freedom and her own beliefs. I want to protect her life. I don't want her to experience a life as her mother did. Now, my life has totally changed.

My Angel gave me hope! I was like a dying flower but now I am alive again and blooming. I am pregnant again and I will have another baby soon. My baby will be an older sister. What a lovely feeling I have!
I hope that this bad experience will not be repeated and hope to have a happy life in a safe place with my kids.

We can't wait for a new dawn when the Othering of us as asylum seekers will stop

Memories of that day still linger and they forever will. Leaving without saying goodbye to my three-year-old son. The guilt of not knowing if he will be taken good care of. Leaving everything behind with just a bag of clothes was the worst time of my life.

I was on a journey of no fixed end. I didn't know where I was going, all l knew was l had to run for my safety. I had sleepless nights, not knowing if l would reunite with my family again. The stress of not knowing if they were all safe because I couldn't communicate with them.

I was on my own, no one to talk to, no one to walk this painful journey with. I feared being sent back from where I was coming from. I had to be resilient and soldier on even though it was very hard.

My life in Direct Provision has been very challenging. Moving from point A to B within a short space of time and just when you think you have settled. I have gone from sharing a room with two other girls from different backgrounds, to sharing a single room as a family of five with a teenage boy and girl. Life has never been the same again.

I feel my kids have lost that sense of security and reliance in me as l have become a child myself. I ask for everything and can't provide for them, contrary to how it used to be back home. My kids are always the newest kid in class as we get moved often, which has paralysed their self confidence. They are drowning in this system and the stigma they get because of staying in DP. It's the simple things that make them feel different from others.

They can't carry proper lunch to school because the centre shop has no provision for that. They walk a distance to school while other kids pass them on the road and it's raining. All these things have affected their confidence. They can't be kids because they can feel this is not their home. This system has stripped us of the last shreds of dignity we had.

We are mentally and psychologically drained. We can't wait for a new dawn when the Othering of us as asylum seekers will stop. When we can be treated the same as everyone else. When we can make use of the education we have. We have a lot to offer, if only we could be given a chance and platform to showcase how talented we are.

My hope is to have a place I call home, to feel safe and live in peace. I hope to be treated fairly and not to be always looked at as the Other person or the asylum seeker. I hope to be given an opportunity to showcase my expertise and prove that I am not here to be a burden of the state but to contribute positively and be a law abiding citizen. I hope my kids' confidence can be rebuilt in future and they live a normal life which empowers them to be who they are and be proud of themselves.

Mi experiencia desde un punto de vista maternal
My experience, from a maternal point of view.

When I was a teenager, the doctors told me that to procreate I would have to do a treatment. I did them, but they were unsuccessful.

After 10 years I came to study English in Ireland, I started a treatment and as a result I got pregnant with twins the day they told me the news, it was one of the happiest days of my life.

However, it was not the same feeling for the father of my babies and he asked me to have an abortion. I told him I think it was wrong, it is not you and I disappeared. All my pregnancy, I was so happy that I did not want anyone to overshadow this wonderful moment as motherhood, I dedicated myself to traveling, working and eating healthy.

They were born super healthy and very big. We were three human beings from one day to the next and as a single mother on the other side of the world, difficult times were coming, despite them being Irish children.

Since they were born, everything was new for me, when I gave birth I had blood loss in the recovery room. That hurt a lot. When I returned to the room with my babies, I felt a very strong pain and joy, such a beautiful feeling to see how wonderful my babies were.

The pandemic has been a disaster for many families and for me it has practically been a blessing because I work from home and I have not missed a single moment of the growth of my little ones.

They are so strong, healthy and happy that as a mother I feel very proud of them, on the street everyone marvels at them because they always have a smile. It is not because I am the mother; they are really adorable

Motherhood as a feeling is the most sublime love that a human being can feel, these children came to teach me to grow and be stronger.

There are so many difficulties in life that one goes through. I can only say that with patience and love, everything can be. I believe the most important thing for the effective development of a baby is that parents transmit love. If they grow in love they will always be loving. From birth up to six years old, they develop their character and it molds their temperament.

I think they do it very well, they are super sociable, creative I even dare to say that they will be very good at sports, they are super active and eat very well.

They began to go to the creche and began to say some words in English, they interact very well with other children but stress they have a special communication

Only 2% of the world's population has twins. I consider myself blessed and very lucky.

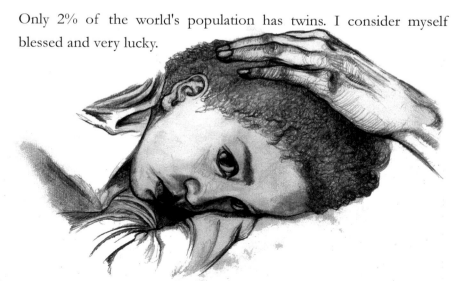

The story of my cat

I came to Ireland in 2015. I was in Balseskin and I was impressed by how Ireland takes care of animals, and how people treat animals like human being. How the pets are important to the family and I just loved that.

Then I move from Dublin to other centre. I was so happy that this centre was open area and there was plenty of cats. I love cats, since I was small, and I was wishing to teach that to my children. It is important to respect animals and take care of them. I had the chance to save three cats at this centre. Lots of cats go missing when they're born, the mother neglects them. It was raining, they were sick and hungry without food.

The cats were female and one male. I named the female Kiki, one male was Missy and the full black male was Billy. So I had the three of them in that place and the management of the Direct Provision centre was happy with that. She saw how good the cats were. They never hurt the children, they do the toilet outside and always come back home. I was showering them and taking them to the vet with the small money I got. I got their food, the vet, all medicine, they were very beautiful. Since 2016 I had them, until 2020. People when they saw the cats, they were shocked. They say, "Look at those beautiful cats!" and they were always happy to see them with me.

They started to be part of my life, part of my heart. My children treat them very well, and they love animals as well. I was proud how they treated the three cats and it was really happy and healthy for everyone.

When I got transferred again, I wasn't thinking about anything. I was only focused on my children and making sure they have a house. I was thinking it was easy to get my cats with me.

The day I leave the centre, I got a cage from people as donation. I put my cats inside and was begging the management to let them come with me. In the end she said, "We can't separate you from them, they are your babies." And I was really happy, I was crying so much. I couldn't leave them behind me.

We take about two hours driving in the bus, they were beside me, I was making sure that they are fine.

Then we came to the home in the new centre and that's where it was a big big problem. The management says to me, "You are not allowed to have cats in this centre."

She came to our home and said, "What is this smell? What is it? No, no, you're not allowed cats!" She was very angry and said, "No way." So she didn't let me talk to her or she didn't ask me or anything.

She called one lady and this lady comes to my home and says to me that she came to collect the cats. I couldn't say no. The law, the power of those people was against me. I couldn't scream, I couldn't. I was shocked. I was crying seeing my cats taken from me. I couldn't believe. I was just crying. I was sick. You know, terrible, horrible feeling.

The lady was nice. She take them to her house and she take care of them and I was contacting her all the time. Sometimes we met outside and she bring the cats in one cage so I can see them. I saw them outside sometimes outside the cage and they was sad. I record them when they was inside the cage and they look sad, they was crying because they want me, and I was crying.

I can't do anything. I can't fight for them. I need my cats in my home because they are mine. The lady couldn't manage with three of them and she gave two away and she keep one. She keep Billy because he's full black and they say in Irish culture having black cat is good luck. And she give Missy and Kiki to a man. The man is very nice. He give me his contact number, he put the cats on warm place and he was feeding them, but they was away from me and I deal with that every day. I couldn't believe and I couldn't stop watching their pictures and videos. I was visiting them regularly.

Then they call me and they say one of the cats are missing. So I didn't see him anymore. Missy is gone. Kiki, she was alive and beautiful and healthy, I was watching her regularly, giving her treats sometimes. So that makes me a little bit happy because she live beside the creche where my daughter is. That's more reason to visit her.

Until the day I go and I ask, "Where is Kiki? I can't see her around" and they say, "Oh maybe she's gone somewhere over there." After that day, they didn't tell me anything until I came back home. They told my husband but they didn't tell me, and I was fasting that day because my religion, we need to fast. My husband let me eat and when I finish eating I was resting and he says to me, "Listen to me, Kiki was found dead on the road."

I put my head on the pillow and I start to scream like crazy. For about one hour I couldn't believe, because before her, the lady who take care of Billy she call me and she say, "I have bad news, Billy has passed away." Can you imagine? Billy is passed away, Missy is disappeared and Kiki is dead, crushed by a car. I didn't say goodbye to any of them.

I didn't see them for the last time. I don't know where is Missy now, so I post in the groups around here to ask if anybody saw him. Just to let me know. Just so I can say goodbye. I don't mind if someone else take care of him, just I want to see him for the last time. Because they are so dear to me.

When they take pets from you, they don't care about emotion. They just think that you're not allowed. You're asylum seeker. You're not allowed to have that. That was big problem for me here. My children were very sad, especially my older girl. She was crying all the time because Kiki was her best friend.

What is left now is just good memories; pictures and videos. I will never forgive them, the people who took my cats away from me because they have pets and when I ask them, "Do you like if your pets are taken away from you?"

They say no, of course.

Why should I feel this? Why am I not allowed to have pets? I don't understand why they do that to me. I'm still crying today for my cats because they were part of my life here as asylum seeker. The only thing that make me happy in that small place.

They wanted us to die, day by day. Maybe we did.

It was hard for me from the first moment I came to Birchwood house. My mother got depressed and she was afraid to be alone (without me). This situation lasted one year. She was stressed from the many doors in the centre. She compared this center with a prison, where there are many doors. She said, "These doors drown me."

When a new resident or family arrives for the first time, the manager says, "If you need anything, don't hesitate to speak with me."

In reality it doesn't happen like this. I understand now, that if the manager knows residents' problems, she can use it to do the worst for them.

Food was very bad. We couldn't eat it. Unwashed salad and raw meat was served to us. When we asked for better food they said, "We can't cook for a particular country." But all countries, culture and religions were unhappy with that food. When we complained about it, chefs said to us, "You came to Europe now and you have to eat what is served here!"

Every resident puts their food in the bin. They survived with food bought from their 19.90€, 21.60€ or 38.80€ social weekly payment. Very often the fruits were finished before we could get them. Adults or children didn't get to enjoy a cake after meals like it happened at other centres. It was lower than the our sum of the budget to get these fruits. It went instead to the manager's pocket. I have seen children crying for ice-cream in front of the chef and their mother. But the chef very quietly said it was finished. It was finished before they could get them.

I can't forget an African guy asking for one more spoon of rice. And the chef with cold blood said to him, 'I don't have enough for all.' He just asked for rice! I was shocked. Really, I was. My heart pained at that moment. I was ready to say to him please take my rice. But I was afraid he would be offended by that. I will never forget that scene. All the world works to raise funds to feed people suffering from famine, and here you are saying I don't have more rice for you.

Residents used to cook in their room to feed their children and themselves. This was a life secret. Just to survive.

The manager found out. After looking at cameras she was ready to check our rooms when we went out, to go to school, or to solve our problems. Secretly she checked rooms and took cookers from residents. Where now could these mothers cook for their children?! Now we have a shop in our center. Sometimes we feel like we are rich or we live in the first class category. This is not from the conditions of our centre, but from the high prices of our food. Rich people can pay more for their food, but their food may be good quality. We have some points, 1 € = 1 Point. These points are very soon finished. Every week we buy something extra from outside shops. Products very often are broken, and when we complain they say, "Maybe it broke in your room?"

I have asked the manager a few times for help. All regarded for my dad's health conditions. He suffers from heart disease. He had high cholesterol, and was going to have a surgery in the heart. I asked the manager if she could change something from the cooked food.

You might ask, "Why did I ask her and not chefs?!"

One time, I heard that a chef said to a resident that he could cook good meals for us, but Manager has a list of foods to be cooked and the way they are cooked. If he would cook well, we might be well fed and might be able to think better and see her dark heart.

Anyway, after I spoke with her she asked me to get a diet plan from the GP to show her. I asked the doctor for it, and she said to me, "I am not a dietitian. But you can print it from the internet!"

I recognised that my problems will not have a solution. I will be like a ball, flying from one hand to another. This doctor didn't refer my dad to a dietitian.

I am happy I learned it after I started college that it was her duty. But what I can do. It is like they can do whatever they want with us. They wanted us to die day by day. Maybe we did.

The favourite thing for the manager was to see residents conflicting with each-other, particularly residents of different origins. I have been in conflict many times for laundry. In the center washing machines are not industrial but home use. They get broken very quickly as they wash 24 hours per day.

Two sisters accused me of removing their clothes out of washing machines before they finished. These sisters were bigger than me. One of them pushed me, she was with her child in her hand. She was using her child to put me in trouble.

61

I called the manager to explain to her the problem. She never listened to what I said to her. The manager never checked the camera when residents had problems to prove what happened. She said to me, "I don't know who's in the right between you."

My conflict was still there. I had to change my walking way, to avoid conflicts with these sisters when they walked the same way. I felt discriminated against and threatened.

When residents needed help from the manager and knocked on her door, her door, she didn't answer. She left residents to wait more than 30 minutes in front of her door. She checked from the camera who was there and didn't open the door.

When a resident didn't know how to complete forms to apply for travel money allowance to go to the hospital in Dublin, he asked the manager. She completed it wrong and he didn't get the money for Social Welfare. They have recognised this problem after the manager did the same problem a few times.

I am sure that there are many other stories which can break hearts. But sometimes people are scared to say them. Maybe they will take them to the grave.

THE NOTES:
LIFE
RACE
DIRECT PROVISION

OTHER
The Projection of the 'Other' and the Intricacies of an Individual's Identity within the Irish Direct Provision System

Sandrine Uwase Ndahiro

OTHERING IN IRELAND

Those that live in Direct Provision, from the moment they arrive on the island of Ireland, are made to feel like an 'Other'. From their arrival, they are made aware of how they are different from Irish citizens. This Other status is a category that is assigned to them to ensure that they know their place within the society. In this category, there is no escape. Within this category, the Other is made to feel like they are wearing a constant sticker on their foreheads that screams 'Asylum Seeker' or 'Refugee'. With this sticker on their forehead, it proves to make life harder, as individuals in Direct Provision are made to feel like they stand out within a public setting.

A brief description of the concept of the Other is needed to understand how this ideology has managed to seep its way through the Direct Provision system and how it is so blatantly obvious, yet again overlooked. This definition of the 'Other' is an ideology that first emerged during the post-colonial era with philosophical thinker Edward Said. In our modern-day society, this is highly visible when you look at the relationship between the West and the 'Third World'.

African individuals from the Third World are often still being viewed as animalistic, backward, and irrational. While those in the West are praised for attaining civility and being rational. This division between the two, therefore, makes it possible to dehumanise the Other. In this case, those who are living in Direct Provision. The individuals are constantly Othered as it is something embedded in our society and we have been turning a blind eye to it for decades.

A distinctive feature that accompanies the ideology of 'Otherisation' is this belief system of 'Us' versus 'Them'. This is a visible feature within the Irish community as it proves to be a sensitive topic when brought up. No one wants to admit that they have subconsciously othered human beings on the basis of things such as race. The use of 'Them' while describing those that live in Direct Provision creates a division within the Irish community. The use of 'Them' desensitises us when it comes to looking at the issue of Direct Provision, as certain people within society still perceive it as a foreign issue as opposed to it being an Irish issue that we all need to tackle.

When it comes to Direct Provision, there is only a general understanding of the highly controversial system. There is a lack of interest in issues happening within crentres across Ireland. Time and time again it is perceived as a foreign issue although it is happening in our hometowns. Once people truly understand and start having conversations about the ideology of Otherisation they will soon begin to understand why it is an issue that needs to be immediately addressed.

When an individual becomes categorised as an Other that individual's voice is silenced, as it ends up being viewed as less important. The voices of those living in Direct Provision are constantly silenced and reduced to background noise. When someone is constantly silenced and made to feel like their voice holds no power, it leads to the individual feeling lesser than. Being placed in a system that does not reassure or encourage individuals to speak out leads to an irreversible trauma that will forever haunt those in the system. Every individual deserves to have their voices heard.

SILENCING VOICES

The silencing of Black voices, or those from minority backgrounds, is a constant feature within our modern-day society. I say this as a person of colour who, from first-hand experiences, is aware of what it means to live in a world where I am constantly silenced and my voice is perceived as lesser than just because of my black skin.

We have been programmed to believe that voice equals power. This understanding of the world has made it an impossible task for those that are constantly silenced on the premises of being an Other to have any sort of power. Within the Direct Provision centres, the voices of those forced to live in these horrendous situations are reminded daily that their voices are not important. Imagine being silenced every moment you raise a concern that has something to do with you or your loved ones. Gaslighting and undermining by managers in centres happens daily. When your voice is taken away, you are truly made to feel insignificant. How can we live in a world blissfully aware that certain people within our shared environment are being silenced and we are not doing anything to help them?

Furthermore, silencing black or minority voices in a predominately white country is not just visible within the Direct Provision centres.

This is visible when it comes to the issue of racism in Ireland. I always notice how people subconsciously place those affected by the system in the category of the Other and immediately disassociates themselves with the issue because they are not affected and it's 'their' problem and not 'mine'. This ignorant view has been adapted in a lot of situations.

An example that immediately sticks out is the ongoing debate of whether racism exists in Ireland. First off, how is this still debatable? Secondly, once again a handful of people are diminishing all the black voices that have now spoken out on their racial encounters in Ireland. Those that have spoken out are being made to feel like they need to prove their racist encounter because their white counterparts have not experienced any racism so they just assume that it is not an issue within Irish society. This is a prime example of 'Otherisation' as people refuse to actively listen to the hardships of those affected by racism and Direct Provision, because it is something that they never have and never will experience due to their privilege. So, now that they can't truly fathom this experience they brush aside and diminish those voices. Just because you do not experience something it does not mean that other members within your society share this.

Modern-day Racism

It is important to point out how the features of Otherisation and the silencing of vulnerable voices within our society are distinctive features of modern-day racism. Racism in the Irish context proves to be a touchy topic due to the incorrect perception of what racism is.

To this day, there is a false understanding of the different categories under the umbrella term of racism. In Ireland, there is a strong belief that we are not a racist country as Black and Irish people do not suffer from the same systematic or institutionalised racism (e.g. police brutality) like those of African American descent across the Pond.

There needs to be an understanding of how racism in Ireland goes beyond the N-word or the institutions previously mentioned. There needs to be a recognition of how the Direct Provision system has racist features in them. In this case, the constant dismissal of individuals in distress whose voices are silenced and replaced with threats and empty promises.

Once again, I ask how can we truly say, as a nation, that we don't harbour racist ideologies? We have predominantly Black and minority populations placed in systems that take away their voice and constantly project Otherness onto them, so we must question this.

It is essential to point out how those that are placed in the category of the Other are always aware of their position in society. In *We can't wait for a new dawn when the Othering of us as asylum seekers will stop,* the writer talks about how they are aware of how they are Othered. Knowing that those around you do not view you as a human being discourages you from using your voice. You are left asking, what is the point if they will never hear me out? This harsh reality of not being treated as a human being proves to be a bitter pill to swallow as you are aware that you may be stuck in this life of the unfair treatment. This heart-breaking reveal strikes a cord, as she is aware that she is treated lesser than just on the mere fact that she is in the Direct Provision system.

Besides, being treated lesser than humans also becomes evident when those in Direct Provision are secluded from the public community. Seclusion from other groups continuously reinforces the concept of the Other. By being separated, the individuals are constantly reminded of how they are overtly classified as different. How is one supposed to integrate into their new community, when the system that you are trapped in continuously perpetuates and encourages this ideology of 'Us' versus 'Them'?

Those in Direct Provision are often unable to integrate with their local community as they are forcibly divided. Once again, it proves to be a difficult concept to understand. Why do we live in a society that consciously divides people, without taking into account the psychological, emotional and traumatic side of being reminded daily that you are different and will never fully integrate into the Irish community?

The fact that someone can confidently identify that they are not viewed as a human being, shows the cracks within our system. Within our modern-day society, this is a heart-breaking eye-opener. Yet, I am not surprised. As a PhD student who specialises in Contemporary African Literature, I have come across endless accounts of films, fiction, anthropology accounts, and travel writings which all talk about how those in the Third World were not viewed as human beings, instead, they were viewed as animals, savages and barbaric due to the colour of their skin.

They were constantly viewed as being sub-human. Those in Direct Provision themselves are aware that they are also viewed as sub-humans. Reading this piece transports me back to my studies as I find it hard to comprehend how something justifiable in the fifteenth century is still relevant in the twenty-first century. How are we still living in a world where vulnerable members of our society are aware of how they are not viewed as human beings? In the sixteenth century, false racial ideologies justified these actions. Yet, we look back at these historical periods with total disgust and view the people with those ideologies as ignorant and archaic.

QUESTIONING OURSELVES AND MOVING FORWARD

I am left with a series of questions. Predominantly, how and why are we still accepting that some individuals are viewed as subhuman? It proves to be an exhausting question to constantly ask why those categorising as an Other automatically just get assigned the role of not being viewed as a human being. If I am feeling frustrated by merely reflecting on my understanding of the inferiority complex, I can't even comprehend the frustrations of the individuals who, day in and day out, are reminded that they will never be viewed as people for as long as they are living in the Direct Provision.

I think that people need to actively educate themselves when it comes to the issue of Direct Provision. The cycle of being self-assigned the role of the Other just for being different needs to be broken down and permanently removed. It is detrimental to move away from our previous silence when it comes to criticizing the system of Direct Provision.

We need to create platforms like this important book that collects stories of Direct Provision where the individuals affected are central to their narrative. This is an integral part that will bring about change giving the vulnerable people in our society their voices back. It is no longer okay to live in a society that places those that are different in the category of the Other.

For change to happen we need to acknowledge how everyone is a valuable member of our Irish society. If we are in the privileged position to shine a light on an individual whose voice has been muffled out, we must take the opportunity. Every person deserves the right to feel dignified and part of humanity. No civilised society should ever make any individual feel less human.

Lastly, Ireland needs to embrace the fact that we are changing and becoming more and more multicultural and diversified as there is no longer one definition of what it means to be 'Irish'. We need to protect those that are the most vulnerable members in our society by actively listening to their daily struggles of life in Direct Provision and actively find ways to make sure that we amplify those voices. Only then can we build a better Ireland where everyone is made to feel like they are valuable members of Irish society and their voices are viewed as important.

Sandrine Uwase Ndahiro

Sandrine is an English Ph.D. student in the University of Limerick. Her research centres on third generation African writers, such as Afrofuturists, who have emerged during the era of late liberalism and who have introduced multiple and nuanced perspectives for reflecting on African lives and aspirations. Sandrine recently co-produced a documentary titled 'Unsilencing Black Voices' which details personal stories and accounts by members of the Black community in Ireland.

Sandrine Recommends:

BOOKS

This Hostel Life by Melatu Uche Okorie

See more of Sandrine's Work:

WEBSITE - www.unsilencingblackvoices.com

www.unapologeticmag.net

INSTAGRAM - @unapologetic_mag

Article originally written for longfordleader.ie 13/03/2021

THE PROBLEM WITH OUR NATIONAL CONVERSATION ABOUT RACISM

The majority of the data collated on the issue of racism in Ireland overwhelmingly suggests that racism not only exists but is having real-world effects on how a great deal of people navigate their lives in our nation.

Eric Ehigie

"Does racism really exist in Ireland?"

The question is one that has frequently been raised since the ascendancy of the Black Lives Matter movement, following the killing of George Floyd in the USA. Floyd's tragic death has forced us to have a long overdue national conversation about racism and the various ways in which it affects people within our country. Although it is principally a positive thing to engage in dialogue surrounding the issue of racism, the premise upon which we are having our conversation is inherently flawed.

The question of whether racism exists in Ireland is not really a question but a well-established axiom. The majority of data collated on the issue of racism in Ireland overwhelmingly suggests that racism not only exists but is having real-world effects on how a great deal of people navigate their lives in our nation.

Consider the following examples. A European-wide study led by Michael O'Flaherty shows that Ireland's rate for racism in the workplace is at 33%. This is up 11% from the EU's average of 22%. Extensive research has also been spearheaded by both the Irish Human Rights and Equality Commission (IHREC) and the Economic

Social Research Institute (ESRI) in the field of racism and discrimination; their Ethnicity and Nationality in the Irish Labour Market study, claims that black Irish people are two times more likely to experience racial discrimination when seeking work, and are approximately four times as likely to be treated in a discriminatory way in the course of their work, than their white Irish counterparts. A more recent collaborative study conducted by the ESRI and IHREC found that when asked directly 66% of the Irish public openly support black migration to Ireland but when respondents are able to conceal their identity and answer with anonymity, only 51% are supportive of black migration. This heralds a more subtle, clandestine form of discrimination.

These are but a few empirical examples of studies that have been conducted in the area, needless to say most of the others point in the exact same direction.

The evidence is stark and unequivocally asserts to the presence of racism in Ireland. Considering this, why is it that our national conversation is solely concerned with questioning the existence of racism and not proposing ways in which we can combat racism and comfort those who are impacted by it? Why are we so unwilling to pay regard to the evidence, which clearly suggests that there is a racism problem in Ireland, that manifests itself in social and institutional ways?

The answer to these questions is surely a multi-faceted one and there probably exists many reasons related to why this is the case; but one major reason of the wider list seems to be the state of denial our nation is in when it comes to merely acknowledging the existence of racism.

For centuries, Ireland has been subjected to a form of colonial racism perpetrated by Britain; expressing itself through the oppressive penal law system, a grueling period of indentured servitude and general subjugation and state violence as a result of religious orientation. Surely if anyone is privy to racism and its cataclysmic effects it is the inhabitants of Ireland who have bore the brunt of racism for so long. Paradoxically, this very history of dealing with racism seems to be one of the seminal causes for our apathy when it comes to addressing the racism faced by so many in our nation. For many, it seems anathema to think that a nation that has had to grapple with racism for so long could ever be accused of perpetuating, let alone possessing, even a modicum of racism.

This denial-ridden way of thinking sees us using our history as a device to exonerate ourselves from the onus of tackling racism, when instead we should be using it as an impetus to empathise with those who confront racism and engage in efforts to combat it. The fact that we are thoroughly aware of the impact racism can have from first-hand experience should implore us to protect those who are currently dealing with racism in our country and, in accordance with the evidence and the stories from people who are experiencing racism, lead efforts to rigorously tackle it – not run away from the collective responsibility to do so.

There also seems to be a general inclination to reference the types of racism present in other countries in an attempt to completely undermine the potency of the racism encountered by people within our own backyard. The "racism only exists in America" assertion is one that is all too frequently utilised whenever attempts are made to kick-start meaningful conversations about the nature of the racism that prevails in Ireland. This relativist approach of juxtaposing Ireland with other nations in the context of racism – or any other societal issue for that matter – to undermine our duty to address racism is inviable, extremely regressive and unsustainable. Take the issue of poverty as an example.

According to the Central Statistics Office, the poverty rate in Ireland as of 2019 was 5.5%. Comparing this to the poverty rate in South Sudan which, according to the World Bank, is currently 82.3%, makes the poverty rate in Ireland seem negligible. Yet, few would dare say – at least publicly – that we should neglect our moral duty to tackle poverty in the best possible way. Such a way of reasoning would be dismissed as absurd.

This way of reasoning could also be applied to homelessness – which is a major problem in Ireland – healthcare and other social issues that our nation faces. Despite the obvious flaws of this relativist approach, we seem to have no problem with applying it to racism; ostensibly allowing ourselves to completely disregard the uniqueness of the racism in Ireland, and to allocate the burden of fighting racism to other nations, instead of rising to the task ourselves.

What our national conversation needs is a complete restructuring. We need to reimagine racism in a manner that is empirically verified and in tune with the sentiments that emanate from people and communities who are most affected by it. We cannot make space for delusion or speculation in our deliberations but must instead, divert our focus to action and the ways in which we can suppress racism. Racism is not an issue that is specific to any one particular community. It is faced by a plethora of different communities; from migrant communities all the way to the travelling community. Therefore, neglecting our collective responsibility to fight it places the burden of dealing with it upon the communities that are impacted by it most. Instead of shying away from our responsibilities, we must own up to the problem of racism and see it as an Irish problem that affects a diverse range of Irish people, which requires a unified Irish effort in order for it to be appropriately addressed.

"We have beyond us the glorious opportunity to inject a new dimension of love into the veins of our civilisation," is what the great Martin Luther King Jr. stated at the zeitgeist of the civil rights movement in the USA. We are at a defining stage in Ireland in terms of race-relations and must choose to inject our national conversation about racism with empathy, realism and a genuine – if utopian – aspiration for a progressive, racism-free Ireland.

Eric Ehigie

Eric Ehigie is a nineteen-year-old student and activist from Longford town. He studies Law and Business at NUI Galway and is the politics coordinator at Black and Irish. Eric hosts the *Engaging with Eric* podcast and his personal YouTube channel, "Eric Osa", and co-hosts the "Political inCorrectors Podcast".

Eric Suggests:

    PODCAST

        Engaging with Eric

        Political inCorrectors

    YOUTUBE

        Eric Osa

See more of Eric's Work:

    WEBSITE - www.blackandirish.com

    INSTAGRAM - @black_andirish / @eric.ehigie

"WHERE ARE YOU REALLY FROM?"

Ethnicity and nationality are not the same thing, even if one person gives the same answer for both questions.

Marica Gunn

Ah, that question. If you are a person of colour who is from a Western country, you have definitely been asked this question. It is aggravating, narrow-minded and racist and I am going to tell you why.

Throughout my life, I have had this question thrown at me on several occasions and some reading this may have even asked others this question and might think nothing of it. On the surface, it may seem innocent, curious and a sign of interest in the other person, as you would simply like to know more about them. That may be true, but when and why you ask it discerns whether you are narrow-minded and racist or appropriately seeking to get more insight into a person's background. This essay will explore why this question (and the various ways in which it is asked) is offensive both when a white person asks this to a person of colour and when the question is asked by a person of colour to another person of colour.

Firstly, this question should never contain the word 'really' as the first offense of this abominable question is that 'really' implies I have lied. One of the several times this occurred is when I was working for Marie Curie in the summer of 2019. I stopped a white man to talk to him about the charity. He then decided, after talking about a terminal illness charity, that the next thing he needed to know was where I was from. I am from London, so I told him that. He did what all racist white people do and said, "Where are you really from?" Thus implying that I had lied when I said London. Why would anyone lie about where they are from to a random stranger, that they will never see again? How is it a lie, when I was born in London, lived there until I was eighteen, have a South London accent (the *Made in Chelsea* one to be exact), have a British Passport...should I go on?

It is so brazen and grotesque to think that you know more about a stranger's life than they do because your racist thoughts dictate so. In actuality, you need to confront why you think a person of colour cannot 'really' be from a Western country.

The second offense of this question has come from a variation. This usually occurs when a white person asks me where I am from and I say London and they then feel the need to say. "Where is your family from," or "Where are your mum and dad from," or even "Where are your grandparents from?"

For the white people reading this who have asked this question: when do you ever require the nationality of a white person's grandparents when you want to find out where they are from? The answer is never, because white people are allowed to be from any place in the world, while people of colour are forced to have our identities confined to Asia and Africa under the laws of white supremacy.

People are allowed to self-define, especially when there is a distinction between nationality and ethnicity. Nationality is how people answer when you ask where they are from, and can often be identified through the country of your first passport (if you have one) or where you were raised. Ethnicity is the country of which shared attributes such as traditions, cultural heritage and religion, come from. Ethnicity and nationality are not the same thing even if one person would give the same answer for both questions. For example, my nationality is British and my ethnicity is Ghanaian, whereas a friend of mine has Irish as her nationality and ethnicity, and my cousin has Ghanaian for her ethnicity and nationality.

When I answer British to this racist question, before they start asking about my entire family tree or utter that ugly word 'really,' I can see the confusion on their faces. It sits like a bee sting, bulbous and unavoidable. In that moment, we are told so much. We are told that you have narrow concepts about identity and probably profess to be one of those people who claims to not be racist, yet cannot accept that people of colour can be from the same place as you. Do you feel threatened? Yes, you do. White supremacy has taught white people to cling onto whiteness no matter what and the idea that any non-white person will share a commonality with them is a threat to their whiteness, a threat which must be stopped.

The duality in my identity is not a threat, it forms all my experiences and I will not ignore one aspect of it so you can feel more comfortable in your racism, and no person of colour should have to do so either. In all honesty, people of colour have no desire to be white, we just want what whiteness grants: humanity, freedom, the power to self-define and to be accepted just as you are.

Lastly, we have covered why this question is racist when white people ask this to people of colour, so we will now explore why it is offensive when people of colour ask this to each other. This happened to me most recently when a black man was supporting me after a racist white woman policed my body. After telling me to pay her no mind, he asked where I was from. I did not perceive this as strange, as it happened in Dublin and my accent is not like any Irish accent, so interpreted his question in that way and said my usual answer and the truth: London. He then asked where my mum was from and I was taken aback as this has not happened in a while, so I said London, asked why we had to go through my family history and walked away. He continued to murmur disbelief at my answers to his white friend.

When this occurs, it is not racist but it is narrow-minded. This usually happens when the person of colour asking the question is the first generation of their family to live outside of the country of their ethnic origin, usually in a Western country.

Therefore, they ask this question to someone of their race to include them in ethnicity. While this may have the best of intentions behind it, the impact is dire. The intent does not acknowledge that even if we are of the same race, we have different experiences and by failing to acknowledge this, they centre themselves and their experiences which reinforces white supremacist teachings. To get the answer that this man wanted, he was expecting me to say the nationality of my great-grandparents because that is how far back in my family tree one would have to go to find people who were born and raised in Ghana, and never left. It is ridiculous to ask where I am from and expect me to speak about my great-grandparents' identities. No one would expect anyone to do that if they were asking about height or food preferences so why does nationality require something different?

Additionally, it would be incredibly ignorant of me to say Ghana when asked where I am from because: (a) I have never lived there so do not have a great concept of life there. I have been on vacation there five times, but I have also travelled to other countries and would not say I am from there, as a vacation does not give you a thorough understanding of a country when you are only there briefly; (b) Through being British, I have benefited from several privileges that family members of mine and numerous other Ghanaians who have never left Ghana do not have. For example, a British passport which makes applying for visas in other countries a lot easier, a posh British accent which people automatically interpret as educated, trustworthy, pleasant, and if I am not seen, people think that I am white so treat me better than if they knew I was black.

To say Ghanaian would be negating these privileges. That should not occur, as part of working towards equality and equity, is knowing where you are positioned in society. I invite you all to do this too if you have not already and hope that this provides insight into similar examples, like when people culturally appropriate another culture and race because their ancestry has 1% of said culture that they are appropriating.

For those white people who are thinking that you are committed to being anti-racist but do want to know about other cultures so want to know how to go about it, the first thing I would say to you is to find writers, creators and artists from other cultures and support their work.

Remember, the next person of colour that you interact with was not put on this earth to educate you. I say this because a racist white man tried to use this as a defense when I said that this question was racist. The issue is that you are still centring yourself at the expense of another as you think that your racist curiosity is more important than a person of colour's ability to self-define. If people of colour want to disclose our ethnicities to you, we will do so when we want to. A friend of mine has dual ethnicity; she is Nigerian and Russian, and how I was informed about this was not through me asking "Where are you from?" I found out through her telling me that she was going to Russia with her mother to see family and that her dad made her Suya (a Nigerian dish) over the weekend.

There is absolutely no need for you to probe us about this within ten seconds of meeting us, and if you feel this need to do so, confront yourself about why that is and work to unlearn it. You have no idea about anyone's relationship with the country or countries that form their identity so do not insinuate we are lying with the answers that we give about our identities. They could be like me, where three generations have lived in England so answering anything besides that would be nonsensical, or could be fleeing their country of origin due to severe trauma associated there (like many people in Direct Provision) and your probing results in them being triggered. In short, accept whatever answer we give or leave us alone so you do not inflict more racist trauma on us.

Marcia Gunn

Marcia Gunn is a writer, activist, dancer and professional wrestler. She also co-hosts Thee Black Frequency on Dublin Digital Radio and is a contributor to The Hush Dialogues. She graduated with a BA from University College Dublin in English Literature and Philosophy, with an extensive focus on critical race theory, intersectional feminism, classism and ableism.

Marcia Recommends:

BOOKS & LITERATURE

The Master's Tools Will Not Dismantle the Master's House by Audre Lorde

Demarginalizing the Intersection of Race and Sex: A Black Feminist Critique of Antidiscrimination Doctrine, Feminist Theory and Antiracist Politics by Kimberlé Crenshaw

Langston Hughes poetry

FILM & POPULAR CULTURE

1. Moonlight
2. If Beale Street Could Talk
3. Pose
4. As Told by Kenya
5. I Can't Breathe by H.E.R. / @hermusicofficial
6. Amandabb

See more of Marcia's Work:

INSTAGRAM - @marciagunn7/ @theeblackfrequency / @hushdialogues

MINDS MATTER IN LIMBO
The mental health considerations of Direct Provision

Dr. Zahra Legris

The number of displaced people in the world has grown in recent decades, placing an increasing number of people in the category of 'refugee'. This term is defined, by the United Nations (and Irish law), as:

> "a person who owing to a well-founded fear of being persecuted for reasons of race, religion, nationality, membership of a particular social group or political opinion, is outside the country of his nationality and is unable or, owing to such fear, unwilling to avail himself of the protection of that country" (UNHCR, 2007).

Such a person, who has left their country of origin to lodge an application for refugee status in another jurisdiction is termed an 'asylum seeker'.

In the Republic of Ireland, the number of applications for refugee status – i.e. the number of documented asylum seekers – rose from 39 in 1992 to 10,938 in 2000 (RIA, 2018). Following this sharp increase, and amidst growing moral concerns regarding the abuse of Irish welfare services (Thornton, 2014), the Irish government introduced policies of dispersal and Direct Provision (Breen, 2008). These policies have become a source of discussion in ethical, legal (Breen, 2008; Thornton, 2004) and political spheres (Ryan et al, 2008), as well as in medical fields (Crumlish & Bracken 2011; CPI, 2017).

The following chapter offers a brief overview of the asylum system in the Republic of Ireland, paying particular attention to the aspects which impact on mental health and wellbeing, as noted in the literature.

It then highlights some of the recommendations by professional and non-governmental organisations of ways to reduce distress, and explores reasons for the lack of published work in this area.

Finally, this piece provides an overview of the volunteer-led groups that are working to advocate and improve the mental wellbeing of those seeking asylum in Ireland. It is aimed at anyone with an interest in mental health and migration, especially those within the medical field who consider themselves advocates for social justice in their work.

DIRECT PROVISION AND MENTAL HEALTH

Direct Provision (DP) is a system of state care which is offered to people who have filed for asylum in Ireland. Whilst their applications are processed, asylum seekers are provided with full board accommodation in Direct Provision centres and a 'Daily Expenses Allowance' of €38.80 per week for adults (Citizens Information, 2021).

Before Ireland joined the EU Receptions Conditions Directive in

2018, there was no legal framework outlining the obligations of the state towards the provision of health services to asylum seekers (Crumlish & Bracken, 2011). They did, however hold the right to access health services, including catchment area mental health services via Community Mental Health Teams (CMHTs).

A dispersal policy adopted by the Reception and Integration Agency (RIA) results in regular resettlement of asylum seekers amongst the 47 centres throughout the country. This makes continuity of care by catchment area mental health services nearly impossible (Crumlish & Bracken, 2011; RIA, 2019).

For those who require mental health intervention, these CMHT's may not be trained or equipped to meet their particular health needs (Crumlish & Bracken, 2011). Moreover, the liminal nature of the DP system on a population of people who are already traumatised appears to worsen their psychological issues (O'Reilly, 2018). Asylum seekers have a 5-fold higher incidence of mental health issues than the average population (Doras, 2020).

The fact that this situation occurs is not only morally questionable, but from a practical perspective is likely to increase the burden on health services. The chances are that by the time they meet a mental health professional within the state services, an asylum seeker's mental health issues will have been compounded by the situation they are living in.

People seeking international protection in Ireland reside in very restrictive conditions. Their autonomy is severely limited – from basic elements such as preparing food at home, to the right and ability to gain employment, the suitability of accommodation (Crumlish &

Bracken, 2011; Doras, 2020; O'Connell et al, 2016).

It can take many years to process an asylum application, during which time asylum seekers in Ireland are not secure in their abodes within the state system. They can be relocated from centre to centre without consultation, whilst facing anxieties that their application could be rejected and they might be deported to an unsafe country of origin. Such policies have been coined policies of deterrence (O'Reilly, 2020; Ryan et al, 2009; Silove et al 2000).

It can take many years to process an asylum application, during which time asylum seekers in Ireland are not secure in their abodes within the state system. They can be relocated from centre to centre without consultation, whilst facing anxieties that their application could be rejected and they might be deported to an unsafe country of origin. Such policies have been coined policies of deterrence (O'Reilly, 2020; Ryan et al, 2009; Silove et al 2000).

Criticism of the DP system has included complaints of promoting child poverty (Fanning & Veale, 2004) and violating the human right to adequate housing (Breen, 2008). In 2017, a working group for the College of Psychiatrists of Ireland (CPI) made a number of recommendations for 'The Mental Health Service requirements in Ireland for Asylum Seekers, Refugees and Migrants from Conflict Zones' (CPI, 2017). One of their recommendations called for a replacement of the DP system with a "more humane, efficient and less traumatising" one (p.6, CPI, 2017). Similarly, the Irish Refugee Council collated a document with a number of local non-governmental organisations (NGO's) categorically stating that the Direct Provision scheme in its present form is discriminatory, and should be abolished (IRC, 2011). A recent brief conducted by human rights group, Doras, outlined the ways that the lack of systematic vulnerability assessments in this group of vulnerable people goes against Ireland's legal obligation to do so under the EU recast Reception Conditions Directive 2018 (Doras, 2020).

The outbreak of the global Covid-19 pandemic has on multiple levels exacerbated the inequalities and inhumane conditions that asylum seekers in DP face. As the whole, world struggled with the uncertainty and undulating restrictions, the general incidence of mental health issues increased up to three-fold. Those already marginalised suffer further (Psychological Society of Ireland, 2020); people living in DP were affected more than the rest of the society around them. As a result of capacity problems in centres, residents were unable to safely socially distance or cocoon (Gusciute, 2020).

They went through an additional layer of isolation in the DP centre setting, as these privately owned centres are often geographically and socially segregated. This, on top of a baseline situation of social exclusion, works to intensify the distress and mental health difficulties that people already face (Doras, 2020; Gusciute, 2020). People suffering from PTSD, complex trauma, mood and anxiety disorders are potentially triggered by being effectively trapped in unfamiliar and, at times, unwelcoming surroundings.

The DP centres are privately owned and managed, and contracted by the Government to implement their reception and integration policies in a commercialised manner (Hewson 2020; Murphy 2021). Despite housing vulnerable groups, it remains unclear how competent managers and staff are at responding to urgent mental health needs. It is imperative that these people are trained to adequately react to such needs (CPI, 2017; Doras 2020) and provided with resources to do so. This responsibility falls under the remit of the Government, who outsource DP centres to enact their own policies. Inadequately governing this process is a 'passing of the buck' at the highest order.

INTERVENING TO REDUCE DISTRESS

As stated above, recommendations have been made by the College of Psychiatrists of Ireland (CPI, 2017), as well as (but not limited to) members of the medical profession (O'Connell et al, 2016), sociologists (O'Reilly, 2020), and human rights group Doras (Doras, 2020) in order to protect the mental health and reduce distress amongst seekers of international protection in Ireland's DP system. Independently of each other, and yet unanimously, these groups call for replacement and dismantling of the DP system as it stands.

Whilst the government has committed to work towards doing so by 2024 (Department of Children, Equality, Disability, Integration and Youth, 2021), there are a number of pressing concerns that ought to be addressed more immediately:

1) Vulnerability assessments for those with mental health conditions or specific needs must be conducted early, and on an ongoing basis. They should be culturally sensitive and accurately informed. This is pursuant to Ireland's legal obligations, and should be informed by those with lived experience as well as health professionals.

2) Health professionals (in General Practice, Emergency Departments, Mental Health Services, Medical and

Obstetric & Gynecology departments) must be adequately trained, supported and resourced to provide appropriate services to this group within their work. This includes, but is not limited to, cultural awareness training, provision of suitable translator services, and assistance to develop targeted outreach services. Moreover, there should be a move towards developing regional specialist refugee mental health teams, which have been recommended by mental health professionals since 2009 (CPI 2017).

3) Managers, staff and responsible people in DP centres should be aware of mental health needs and trained in how to respond to crises. They should also be required to implement the recommendations that qualified health professionals make to alleviate distress and promote wellbeing.

Certainly, recommendations 1) and 2) apply, even with the aforementioned commitment from the Irish Government to phase out the current system and implement a "New ethos for the International Protection Support Service" (p.42, Department of Children, Equality, Disability, Integration and Youth, 2021). Culturally informed, context-appropriate assessments and health service provision are relevant no matter what system is in place.

Unrepresented

These recommendations are important and achievable, however, the data required to propel them into action are lacking in published works. There are very few longitudinal studies pertaining to the mental health and psychosocial wellbeing of asylum seekers (Ryan et al 2009).

The prevalence of cross-sectional studies amongst small, heterogeneous populations is likely due to one or more of the following factors; their lack of inclusion on systemic lists, high degree of geographic mobility (particularly within countries which have policies of dispersal), high levels of linguistic and cultural diversity, lack of funding and government reluctance, or fear and mistrust of authority figures amongst this population (ibid). Additionally, there exists a relatively high level of shame and stigma surrounding mental health issues amongst many in this group.

Another reason that researchers may be reluctant to study this population, relates to the perceived vulnerability of asylum seekers and the resultant implications for ethical approval procedures.

Vulnerability amongst research populations is a contested issue within the field of research ethics (Bracken-Roche et al, 2017). The intention of guidelines is usually to protect those at increased risk of stigmatisation (Delor & Hubert, 2000) or harm through participation, or those who are assumed to have impaired autonomy (Finnegan & O'Donoghue, 2017).

In the Irish setting, asylum seekers exhibit a spatiotemporal experience of vulnerability (Watts & Bohle, 1993). They hold vulnerabilities amidst issues of entitlement, but also through powerlessness in their context.

As we have understood, the system of Direct Provision is likely to compound such vulnerabilities or bring to light additional ones in the form of restricting autonomy and agency (Breen, 2008; Crumlish

& Bracken, 2011), making this group subject to multiple and cumulative vulnerabilities (Cannon, 1994; Pedersen 2002; Watts & Bohle, 1993). Accordingly, asylum seekers in Ireland hold extrinsic vulnerabilities relating to dependence on the state for food, shelter, clothing and other basic human needs. They may also hold intrinsic vulnerabilities, depending on their mental health status and psychosocial stress and social conditions.

Notwithstanding these vulnerabilities, it is important that such groups be involved in mental health research as their participation has been instrumental in reducing gaps in evidence-based care (Finnegan & O'Donoghue, 2017). Research Ethics Committees (RECs) engage mostly in aspects of research that will directly benefit participants (ibid).

Despite this restriction, it is hoped that having a platform to make one's voice heard will be a positive and empowering experience for members of a population lacking social and institutional engagement opportunities (MacDonald et al, 2013); particularly if the research focuses on a area in which participants' health outcomes can be closely entwined with socio-political aspects of their environment, such as mental health.

The apparent paucity of published work in this area is problematic on a number of levels; policy making is largely evidence based, particularly in the health field. Lack of qualitative or quantitative data means that these important issues are made invisible, therefore crucial changes cannot occur. Moreover, it could be ventured that in bearing witness to injustices such as those faced by those living in DP in Ireland, one has a moral duty to give people a voice.

WHAT CAN WE DO TO CHANGE THINGS?

For the most part, volunteer-led organisations attempt to fill the gaps in provision of adequate state mental health services by raising awareness, providing advocacy and developing psychosocial interventions. These groups include (but are by no means limited to):

- **Cairde** (Irish for *friend*) is a community development organisation working to tackle health inequalities among ethnic minority communities by improving ethnic minority access to health services, and ethnic minority participation in health planning and delivery. Cairde aims over the next three to four years to implement actions which will be seen to have a measurable impact on the delivery of primary health care to a selected number of disadvantaged ethnic minority communities in Dublin.

- **AkiDwA** – Akina Dada wa Africa-AkiDwA (Swahili for *sisterhood*) – is a national network of migrant women living in Ireland. AkiDwA's vision is a just society where there is equal opportunity and equal access to resources in all aspects of society – social, cultural, economic, civic and political. Our Mission is to promote equality and justice for all migrant women living in Ireland. AkiDwA consults with migrant women and other key stakeholders, identifies discriminatory practices and develops evidence-based and representative solutions that address key issues like health, sexual and gender-based violence, and discrimination.

- **The Danú Project** is a volunteer-led organisation which supports asylum seekers and newly integrated refugees through three core projects:
  - Pregnancy and Maternity Kits;
  - Youth Engagement and Development;
  - Mental Health Support.

Projects are discussed with people seeking asylum to ensure they reflect the genuine needs of those affected.

Representatives living in DP ensure voices are heard from throughout the system so even the most vulnerable are reached and supported. The Mental Health Project continues to grow based on expressed needs and the skills-set of volunteers. It aims to provide a safe space with a sense of community, raise awareness about mental health difficulties and provide psychosocial support.

- **Spirasi** (Spiritan Asylum Services Initiative) is the national centre for the rehabilitation of victims of torture in Ireland. The rehabilitative services offered by Spirasi are unique in Ireland and consist of the following:
  - Multidisciplinary (medical, therapeutic and psychosocial) Initial Assessment (IA) for both victims of torture and those who have suffered cruel and inhuman or degrading treatment;
  - Ongoing therapeutic interventions for victims of torture which includes individual, group and family therapies;
  - Both in-house and outreach psychosocial supports;
  - Medical Legal Reports (MLRs) for the protection process;

- English language classes for victims of torture and their families that complement the rehabilitative work.

- **Doras** is an independent, non-profit, non- governmental organisation working to promote and protect the rights of people from a migrant background in Ireland. Their vision for Ireland is a society where equality and respect for the human rights of migrants are social norms. Their mission is to promote and uphold the human rights and well-being of migrants through personal advocacy, integration development and collaborative advocacy campaigns at the local and national level.

On an individual level: support, volunteer or donate to those accepting donations. It is important to raise awareness of the DP system and educate oneself and others. Bring these lessons and reflections into your workplace or academic space.

This could occur in various ways; educators must inform their students or platform voices of asylum seekers in a sensitive manner. Health professionals should advocate for this group, as is their mandate. They should also work with their supervisors and colleagues to create evidence bases that are lacking, or develop policies around the care of asylum seekers. Legal professionals and public sector workers are likely to be able to identify aspects of their work where the aforementioned gaps can be filled. Artists can, and often do, find ways to use their platforms for awareness and fundraising.

Doing these things with purpose and integrity requires asking the hard and unpopular questions; of yourself, of your family, your workplace, your managers, your TD. It involves paying attention and giving visibility to hidden aspects of our society.

At the very least, engaging with this involves being on the right side of history when it comes to the one of the great moral tests of our time; the rights and treatment of those seeking safety under international protection.

Dr. Zahra Legris

Zahra is a Psychiatry trainee, activist and mental health advocate. She has a passion for social justice and works hard to bring this into her professional and charity endeavours. She obtained her medical degree from Trinity College Dublin. Zahra has a MSc in Global Health and Social Justice from King's College London, where her dissertation focused on NGO Mental Health Interventions in the occupied Palestinian territories.

CLIMATE CHANGE MIGRATION NEXUS

It is vital to remember that climate migration is not a future risk. It is a very present reality that demands immediate attention and response. To say that climate change directly causes movement or displacement is, however, a vast oversimplification.

Caoimhe Durkan & Cormac Nugent

We are currently facing what Doctors Without Borders has described as 'the worst displacement crisis since the Second World War'. At the same time, we are bearing witness to environmental collapse and an ever-increasing rate of extreme weather events. Climate change is often described as an existential risk, one of the greatest threats facing humanity right now. While global environmental change and climate breakdown affects each and every one of us, it does not do so in equal measure.

According to the 2020 Ecological Threat Register, the decades since 1960 have seen the frequency of natural disasters increasing tenfold, resulting in the displacement of approximately 25 million people in 2019 – almost triple the 8.6 million that were displaced as a result of armed conflict. By 2050, it is estimated that climate change will create "up to 86 million additional migrants in sub-Saharan Africa, 40 million in South Asia and 17 million in Latin America".

However, it is vital to remember that climate migration is not a future risk. It is a very present reality that demands immediate attention and response. To say that climate change directly causes movement or displacement is, however, a vast oversimplification.

Rather, its effect has been described as amplifying and intensifying pre-existing social, political, economic, and environmental issues. It further complicates and exacerbates problems in communities that are already facing resource scarcity, conflict, overpopulation, weak infrastructure, bad governance and/or environmental vulnerability. In many cases, it becomes the match in a powder barrel.

The true scale of how climate change affects migration is difficult to measure for a variety of reasons. One of these being that, while we may be able to estimate the number of people that are displaced as a result of sudden onset natural disasters, such as typhoons, hurricanes, flooding and wildfires, many people will also migrate as a result of slow onset environmental changes, such as sea-level rise, desert-ification and biodiversity loss, among others.

In addition, environmental changes can have direct social, political and economic consequences with poorer countries often more vulnerable to the negative impacts of environmental disruption.

Communities experiencing conflict or socio-political tensions may also be further at risk. Experts indicate that resource scarcity can exacerbate existing tensions, and warn that food and water shortages can be exploited by terrorist groups. In addition, many communities on the frontlines of climate change are those that have been actively 'underdeveloped' by countries in the global north through colonialism.

Not all environmental migrants are refugees, and experts have suggested that the continued use of the term 'climate refugee' does not serve the interests of those in need of protection. This is because this term refers to very specific legal rights and protection, and its misuse may actually undermine the rights and protection of traditional refugees.

Contrary to what many people might think when they hear of 'climate-induced migration and displacement,' such movement is usually internal. In the majority of cases, most people migrate within their own country. In spite of this, many media outlets continue to fixate on movement that occurs across international borders, and frame climate migration as a future 'threat'. Indeed, as highlighted by François Gemenne and Caroline Zickgraf "floating the prospect of a looming migration crisis is only likely to fuel current xenophobic prejudices against migrants and refugees."

The same media groups (right wing) who emphasise, exacerbate and at times formulate the negative impacts of global migration are those who have questioned for decades the legitimacy of climate scientists and the indisputable existence of man-made climate change itself. The fear trumped-up through negative stories and the parading of non-experts by these morally corrupt media organisations has in the past stoked tensions across the world during previous times of mass migration including the time following the Syrian Civil War. A caveat to this example being that climate change, expressing itself through the worst drought in 900 years, worsened the conditions that eventually led to this brutal conflict and the resulting 6.6 and 6.1 million externally and internally displaced people respectively.

What needs to be done?

1) Achieving the Paris Agreement's ambitious goal of keeping global temperature increases to below 1.5 degrees Celsius. The cornerstone of mitigation is to reduce global emissions and thus lessen the impacts of climate change and future extreme weather events.

2) Create pathways for climate migrants through several avenues including, as Jane McAdams has articulated, 'enhancing voluntary migration opportunities; developing humanitarian visas; and potentially even undertaking planned relocations, in full consultation with affected communities', the final statement being absolutely essential. It's important to recognize that while climate change impacts could force many people to move, it can also trap people in dangerous situations. Safe pathways and flexible migration programs must be created to assist those affected by environmental disruption to remove themselves from such situations.

3) Ensure accurate and compassionate reporting from both the media and government officials/institutions, of the genuine causes and impacts of migration. This however will prove more difficult due to the polarised views between media organisations, the pervasiveness and the algorithmically enhanced divisions in social media discussions.

The Paris Agreement with the overall ambition of halting global temperature increases below the 1.5C threshold, fought for by small island nations (who will and already are being disproportionately impacted by climate change), holds within it detailed, although some argue unambitious, global cooperation and supports necessary to enable adequate adaption and mitigation ensuring the protection of potential climate migrants. The relationship between climate change and migration is one that is far too complex to fully outline within the constraints of a single article. Nevertheless, it is a connection that cannot be ignored.

What we hope to achieve is to provide a starting point for you, the reader, to reflect and research. We hope to see radical change in our society in the way we think about and treat migrants, refugees, and asylum seekers, alike. That we will do away with the cruel, dehumanizing systems currently in place, and welcome all with warmth, compassion and respect.

Caoimhe Durkan

Caoimhe is a freelance filmmaker, photographer and writer, and a contributor with ClimateLoveIreland. She has been engaging with environmental issues for a number of years - through involvement with various campaign and action groups (in the UK, Australia and Ireland) as an undergraduate and after college, and in the form of freelance environmental writing and reporting. She is a firm believer in the power of written and visual storytelling to provoke questions, open conversations, shift and challenge perceptions, and incite positive action. She is currently studying an MA in Ethnography and Documentary at University College London.

Caoimhe Recommends:

BOOKS

Climate Justice by Mary Robinson

Hope in the Dark by Rebecca Solnit

The Uninhabitable Earth by David Foster Wallace

On Fire by Naomi Klein

This Changes Everything by Naomi Klein

PODCAST

Mothers of Invention

Displaced Podcast by Rescue.org

Outrage and Optimism

The Yikes Podcast with Mikaela Loach and Jo Becker

Hot Take – Mary Annaïse Heglar and Amy Westervelt.

See more of Caoimhe's Work:

Instagram: @kivadurkan / @kiva_durkan

Cormac Nugent

Cormac is a climate activist, writer and advocate for positive climate action. He is a contributor to the ClimateLoveIreland Blog and Instagram account. Recently, Cormac completed a masters at Dublin City University in Climate Change, Policy, Media and Societal Transition and is currently seeking employment in this field. Cormac loves spending time in nature and the recent pandemic has made him realise again how important it is for everyone's mental and physical health.

Cormac Recommends

PODCAST & DOCUMENTARY

A Life on Our Planet & Our Planet by David Attenborough

Climate Queens Podcast

BOOKS

Climate Justice by Mary Robinson

On Fire by Naomi Klein

The Future We Choose: Surviving the Climate Crisis by Christiana Figueres and Tom Rivett-Carnac

SOCIAL MEDIA

@climateloveireland

@theuselessprojec

See more of Cormac's Work:

WEBSITE - www.climateloveireland.com

INSTAGRAM - @cormacnugent / @climateloveireland

THE EU RECEPTION CONDITIONS DIRECTIVE

How Ireland fails to meet the standards of the reception rights for applicants of international protection as established by the EU.

Paula Martinez

In 2013, the EU Reception Conditions Directive was created to establish standards of the reception rights for applicants of international protection. Ireland has to follow certain standards that the European Union puts in place for different aspects of life, and the reception standards for applicants of international protection is one of them. However, since joining in 2018, Ireland has failed to follow many of the regulations they signed up to.

The Directive defines an applicant as 'a third-country national or a stateless person who has made an application for international protection in respect of which a final decision has not yet been taken'. Applicants have the right to be clearly informed of their rights within the country they are seeking asylum, yet Ireland is doing a poor job of informing its applicants of their rights as many testimonies reveal these needs are not met.

The Directive clearly states in Article 5(1-2) that member states need to provide very clear information to their applicants about their established benefits and obligations relating to reception conditions and information on groups and organisations that provide legal assistance or help them; this information should be provided in writing or verbally, if needed, to the applicant and should come in a language the applicant can clearly understand. It is clear that Ireland is not informing its applicants effectively, or they are denying them of their rights even when the applicants know what they are entitled to. In the next paragraph I will explain how, by the directive's standards, it makes no sense why these applicants are denied the right to work or the right to cook, and how both of these rights are connected to people's dignity, something which has to be protected and facilitated for applicants anywhere in the world.

Even if the state says those rights are guaranteed, there are many testimonies showing the lack of will to inform applicants of their rights and the lack of an avenue to allow applicants to enjoy their rights while they wait for a response. This is, in itself, a violation of the Directive. It is inhumane for countries to agree to standards written to protect people from human rights violations in their countries of origin and then not act on what they agreed to do. Such action ends up playing with people's mental health and dignity.

Countries that live in peace and balance have a duty to provide protection for a certain number of people from countries where there are consistent human rights violations. With industrialisation, mechanisation and globalisation we are living in a world that is completely connected, and it is possible to travel the globe. This has created a necessity for global decrees and regulations for migration and applicants of international protection status. These decrees and regulations are in place to provide order and a controlled environment for people needing aid, which helps maintain balance and order in the country receiving them. They also protect migrants and international protection applicants from human rights abuses, not only when they are accepted into a new country, but also while they are waiting for a response to their application.

Applicants for international protection who are waiting for an answer still try to live their lives, and most of the time the waiting process takes years. This is why decrees and regulations to protect them during this process are so important. Even though by the law applicants are at a standstill, in practice their lives are not, and in failing to meet certain basic standards the country receiving applicants might be violating their human rights for years while they wait.

A very clear example of this is how Ireland did not comply with the 2013 Directive until 2018. By not doing so for many years, Ireland did not allow its applicants awaiting a response from the state the right to work. This was against EU law. Ireland had to be taken to court by a Burmese man in order for this to be modified and then it was found that Ireland needed a radical change because applicants deserve their right to work. EU law states that after nine months of being in the country and in the protection status determination process, without an answer, asylum seekers must have the right to work.

The right to work in the case of the Burmese man vs Minister of Justice and Equality (N.H.V and F.T.V. The Minister for Justice and Equality (Respondent) and the Irish Human Rights Commission (Notice Party) is directly linked with poverty, dignity and self-worth. This is not anything you should make people go through if you meet the basic reception standards for applicants.

The right to work has been accepted by numerous international human rights organisations as one of the most essential basic rights all people deserve access to. The right to work is vital, as it is the base from which to access many other human rights, and it is 'inseparable' from human dignity. Not only this, but it is also closely linked to being able to provide a dignifying life for your family. Earning a living is closely linked to self-worth and personal growth and also recognition and connection with your community. Not only are Direct Provision crentres breaching the 2013 EU Directive standards, but they are also breaking universal human rights laws when not allowing applicants to work. While Ireland has recently changed the right to work laws for asylum seekers, there still remain barriers that are left unattended.

For example, the remote location of many centres make it unrealistic to find work and there can be language barriers. The state does not provide solutions for these.

The Directive of 2013 says that material reception conditions, which include food, have to be of a good, living standard for applicants. Many centres provide poor catering only, and no cooking facilities for an alternative. I do not believe this complies with what the 2013 Directive writes on material reception conditions. It makes no sense for the state to pay for catering to provide food for international protection applicants and not provide cooking facilities. It makes no sense for applicants not to having the right to cook their own meals and it clearly has shown it goes against basic concepts of dignity and respect towards human beings.

There have been numerous complaints to the state and media about the food quality and quantity in Direct Provision crentres. Not only is it an insult not to allow someone the basic right to cook for themselves, but it is also ridiculous to assume a large number of people (that do not know each other, from different countries and religions) would like to eat the same food. The food from Direct Provision is not only culturally insulting and insensitive to different religious needs, but also has been proven to be bad for applicants' health, and unsuitable for babies and toddlers. This clearly shows how it goes against the living standards for applicants set by the 2013 Directive.

Everything is connected when it comes to Direct Provision and the centres' lack of respect for human rights. If applicants were to be treated correctly under basic reception standards, they would be immediately informed about their work rights. They would also be facilitated by different programs to find work after the appropriate time had passed. This would be necessary to have in place to increase equity.

Applicants are at a disadvantage in finding work compared to other citizens in Ireland. because of language, cultural shock, lack of connections, and many more factors. Applicants provided with the right to work would easily be able to have better quality food through their income and they could decide what they want to eat. The right to work would grant applicants agency. But even then, Direct Provision has to provide facilities for them to cook and be able to eat with dignity.

Paula Martinez

Paula is a Brazilian-Ecuadorian MA student, studying Asylum Law, Racism and Migration Issues. She came to Ireland aged seventeen and did an undergraduate course at University College Dublin in Politics and French. Paula strongly believes that the mentality of the State and that of societies receiving migrants needs to change. Education for native people needs to focus on understanding the value of diversity for their countries. Programs need to be created that allow migrants and people seeking protection to blossom in their new country, and allow them to be actors of change.

See more of Paula's Work:
WEBSITE - www.danuproject.ie
INSTAGRAM - @chocolatecalienteconchile / @thedanuproject /
@hushdialogues

A LETTER FOR YOU; A PLEA TO IRELAND
Addressing the conditions of those living in Direct Provision.

Ciara Curtin

To any individual reading this, who lives in the Direct Provision system, I first and foremost want to express my extreme rage and frustration at those in the Irish government. The way people, like yourself, are treated and represented in this country makes me feel completely ashamed to be from here. Your life matters, just as much as the next person. Your health and wellbeing matter, just as much as the next person.

In these difficult times I can understand that your hope and trust in any person is diminished. If anything, I want to tell you that this will not go on for much longer. We will be representatives; we will continue to fight for what is right and to end Direct Provision centres nationwide.

The younger generation of adults in Ireland are all about positive change. We have seen many things change in this country over the last number of years, things which we never believed would happen. Our next mission is to end Direct Provision centres. While I can't even imagine what you live through every day, I yearn that you will end up living a life of freedom, a life where you don't need to think about holding onto one more day because your dreams will become reality.

When it comes to the issue of Direct Provision, I am always left with a million questions that have never been addressed. One being, how can we as a country allow this injustice to happen? My anger lies with the Irish government.

As a country we agreed to provide refuge for those seeking it. The government agreed that it would provide shelter, food and safety from those fleeing from extremely impoverished countries and critical circumstances. It absolutely disgusts me and I refuse to believe that this is what protection and welcome means in Ireland.

Personally, I have lost faith in the system, as time after time excuses are being made as to why Direct Provision still exists in Ireland. We need to shout louder and refuse to continuously turn a blind eye on this issue which is slowly crippling the voices of the most vulnerable in Ireland. We need to remain resilient and promise to never give up fighting for those whose voices have been hushed and shunned and have been denied the chance at living a normal life. If we can't fight for this, nobody else will. This government has proved to be incompetent when it comes to the need of addressing the issue of Direct Provision. They have hoped that this issue will go unnoticed and let it slide by. A way of raising an issue and letting it slide by, hoping that no one will have noticed what was brought up. This needs to end. It may seem like an impossible task but, by merely refusing to remain silent when it comes to seeing other voices suffer in silence is the first step for change.

For those of you reading this who are new to all this, you must be here for a reason. You likely care and are looking to expand your knowledge and learn how to actively care. We need to realise what asylum seekers and refugees are living and have lived through, to understand that this is their reality. A reality that sees us become desensitised to the inhumane treatment that they are being subjected to. A reality where a chance for freedom and integration into the Irish community is a far fetched idea; an unattainable dream.

I find it extremely difficult when I encounter people who still do not understand or believe the inhumane nature of Direct Provision. For years, people have just believed a lie constructed by those in power about these centres. Direct Provision is seen as something that is just and fair from the point of view of the Irish government.

The country has committed to taking in individuals fleeing persecution and provide them with protection, but the reality is that this 'protection' is inhumane. Those living in Direct Provision are fearful of a multitude of things such as health, financial security as well as mental wellbeing. Their only other option is to leave the facility that they have been brought to but if they do that, they're out on the streets. This notion baffles me.

How is it 2021 and the government supports either involuntary imprisonment or being another statistics of the homeless on the streets? No one should be punished for seeking a safer life. At night, an asylum seeker might lie awake, wondering which option is better. One option they are left to ponder on is whether it is actually better living on the streets, where at least there is a sense of freedom. Hypothetically the person would be able to walk around, smell the fresh air and be somewhat in control of their own life. However, it is important to highlight how either option sees the individual's sense of humanity being chipped away. While being homeless, a person won't have any place to rest their head at night, they won't have money to spend on any food or essentials; there won't be any sense of security.

In these horrendous centres, you're staying with other families, have very little privacy and are provided with inadequate food. Something as small as having your own room or being able to prepare your own meal and have some control of your circumstances is prohibited in these centres. Adult asylum seekers receive an extremely low amount of welfare at €38.80 per week. This is meant to cover supplies and essentials needed to live each day for them and their families.

To a lot of us who might be dipping into the realities of Direct Provision for the first time, reading and learning something like this just doesn't seem real. How is it that in the 21st century we are allowing something like this to happen, to people who have as much right to live here as anyone else?

However bad our struggles may be in life, most of us aren't treated inhumanely just because of where we come from and what our social status is. The people living in Direct Provision centres did not ask for any of this. They were told that there was a one-way ticket out of their country; they did not know that the ticket they would be receiving would bring them into another hellish reality. A reality where they are constantly fighting for the chance to be treated as human beings.

Direct Provision crentres are our present-day Mother and Baby Homes, there is no denying that. When will we look at the Direct Provision centres and feel the same sense of dismay? How far does this need to go until all the people of Ireland can stand up and fight to abolish these horrendous conditions?

Likewise, I can't tell you how ashamed I am to have only learned about Direct Provision centres within the last two years. I can't tell you how even more ashamed I am that I thought that these centres were beneficial and were a stepping stone for those who were brought here. I can hold my hands up and admit that I never educated myself about this topic thoroughly until last year. But once I researched, I then knew what was happening there and took it upon myself to spread awareness and further educate others on this matter.

I'm in a position of being educated on the topic and now want to ensure that those around me become knowledgeable about the issue too. I can't stress how important it is to learn about what is happening to asylum seekers in our country every single day. People can spend up to seventeen years living in Direct Provision.

Seventeen years is a very long time to live in a system that sees you as lesser than, as subhuman. This is something that I cannot even fathom. The implications of staying in a place like this, especially for a long length of time, can have a big impact on somebody's physical and mental wellbeing.

When I began my research, I went in with the idea that this was a good environment for asylum seekers to be in and wondered what the problem was. As I delved deeper into the internet and looked up articles, tweets and stories I became shocked and saddened about what I was reading, this including the abundance of negativity and ignorance.

We are all humans who are just looking for ways to survive on this earth, we aim to live contently and safely. It's really important to ask yourself questions when educating yourself to understand why it is necessary to understand and abolish Direct Provision. Questions such as; why have we created this division with each other based on where we come from, our social class or even the colour of our skin? Who has instilled this divide upon us to make us think and act in such a way to those from all parts of the world?

Equality for all will not affect you in any negative way. I encourage everyone to see past concerns which have been created by superiors to get us to ignore the real problem here; asylum seekers living in poverty. The problems, those with doubt have manifested, lie with asylum seekers who have done nothing to affect them personally or have changed anything within their own life. However, the problem shouldn't be directed at asylum seekers, it is with the government who are keeping this type of institution alive. It's time to shift your attention to who the real opponent is. By educating ourselves on various platforms such as spunout.ie, nascireland.org or even by talking to one another on Facebook, Instagram or Twitter we can be what is needed to end this 'temporary accommodation' for good.

Let's make sure we work with each other, not against, to bring an end to Direct Provision. Contact your local TDs and keep getting them to raise this issue in Dáil Éireann until it's over.

Ciara Curtin

Ciara Curtin is currently studying a MA in Post-Primary Education (English and History) at Hibernia College Dublin. Having completed a CELTA qualification she worked as an English language teacher in Dublin. It was in this setting that she experienced working in an inclusive environment with a range of diverse students. Since then, Ciara is keen to develop awareness and achieve equal human rights here in Ireland. She believes there is a need for education in secondary schools about racism and discrimination.

Information and contact details for your local TDs can be found at www.oireachtas.ie

THE QUESTION OF IRISH NEUTRALITY
Where Ireland really stands in international politics and relations.

Yara Alagha

Ireland's neutrality is not enshrined in the Constitution, in law, or in any international treaty. It is a one-line policy statement with no detail nor legal underpinnings. Even the term 'neutrality' masks quite a complicated and multifaceted concept, one that is ambiguous to some and essential to others. And although Ireland will never be a military coalition partner in any coalition conflict, it has been an active perpetrator and bystander of the greatest atrocities to unfold in the modern era.

In 2001, following the attacks of September 11, Ireland's Taoiseach Bertie Ahern flew to America to offer President George W. Bush the unlimited use of Shannon Airport in an invasion of Afghanistan. Since then, Ireland has played the role of controversial accomplice in America's 'War on Terror.' Each year, hundreds of thousands of U.S. troops land in Shannon while their planes fill up on fuel and supplies. And each year, new accusations surface of CIA rendition flights passing through Ireland on their way to torture camps scattered around Europe. Shannon Airport has been used in the invasions and occupations of Iraq and Afghanistan, and in the illegal rendition circuits operated by the CIA.

The practice, as currently implemented, is not consistent with the responsibilities of a neutral country under the Hague Convention V on Neutrality 1907. The Convention states that "belligerents are forbidden to move troops or convoys of either munitions of war or supplies across the territory of a neutral Power." Even though Ireland hasn't ratified the Hague Convention, a 2003 High Court judgment in Horgan v An Taoiseach et al. stated that the state was in breach by allowing US troops to use Shannon on their way to and from war in Iraq.

Shannon Airport has also been identified as a stopover point in the US government's extraordinary rendition programme. On 22 July 2002, a US private aircraft was recorded to have stopped over in Shannon Airport, on its return journey to the US after taking UK resident Binyam Mohammed to Morocco where he was tortured. Binyam was subsequently detained without charges in Guantanamo Bay between 2004 and 2009.

For far too long we have been complicit in the deaths and torture of countless innocent civilians. This must change by withdrawing landing rights in Ireland from all US military and CIA flights.

IRELAND AND THE UIGHUR GENOCIDE

China's wolf-warrior diplomacy, coupled with its ability to leverage its economic power to mitigate any scrutiny of its crimes against humanity, perhaps plays a role in Ireland's position of shying away and bowing down to China's diplomacy. But, can we forgive Ireland's complicity in the genocide? Absolutely not.

I want to make sure we frame the current treatment of Uighur

Muslims right: it's a genocide. It's detention camps; arbitrary incarceration of more than three million Muslims without trial or conviction; the harvest of organs; the exploitation of labour; the forced separation of children from their families; and the forced sterilisation of Muslim women.

The BBC published a report on the systemic rape of female detainees in China's 'reeducation camps.' Former detainees and escapees recount the organised mass rape perpetrated by the Chinese police personnel. Ziawudun, who fled Xinjiang after her release and is now in the US, recalls women being removed from the cells every night and raped by one or more masked Chinese men. She said she was tortured and later gang-raped on three occasions, each time by two or three men. We know from testimonies submitted to the Uyghur Human Rights Project that women are subjected to barbaric forms of torture including electrocution through 'anal rape with a stick'. Birth rates declined by more than 60% between 2015 and 2018 in Uighur regions of Hotan and Kashgar, the AP found.

When I first heard about what was happening to Muslims in China in 2017, I was a student at UCD. On my daily commute through the grounds of Belfield, I walked past the construction of the new 'temple-style' and modern-glass Confucius Institute. It's one of two Institutes in Ireland and many around the world which serve to strengthen cultural and education ties. Many of these institutes have been shut down globally in European states and universities in recent years such as in Sweden and Germany, who cite growing concerns of Chinese influence and propaganda.

Co-financed by UCD, the Irish and Chinese governments, both

Irish parties signed the agreement with Hanban, the world headquarters of Confucius Institutes and also the public relations wing – better known as its propaganda wing – of the Chinese Ministry of Education. This is the same body and ministry that is overseeing and orchestrating human rights violations and abuse against Uighur Muslims and other Muslim minorities in China.

While the Irish government celebrated and launched the Institute in 2018, with our fifth largest trade partner, and celebrated its 40th year of diplomatic Sino-Irish relations the following year in 2019, a genocide shrouded in secrecy was being committed in the backdrop. While we continue to weak-needly prioritise our diplomatic relations, we continue to condone the legal system for arbitrary detentions and disappearances, continued widespread use of torture, forced organ harvesting, and sterilisation of Uighurs.

Why should Ireland care for injustices happening so far away when we've got crises of our own? When I listen to reports of Uighurs subjected to barbaric physical and psychological abuse happening now, in real-time, as I write and as you read this piece, I think to myself: in 100 years time when this is written in the history books and we read back on this dark time for Uighurs in horror, will history vouch for us, for Ireland? Will it reassure our future children that we stood against genocide, and when we said "never again" to past injustices, that we meant it?

THE OCCUPATION OF PALESTINE: IRELAND STANDS CLOSE BUT IDLE

Palestine has long occupied a place in Irish consciousness with a unique transnational solidarity resulting from historic parallels between the Irish and Palestinian struggle under settler colonialism. Seldom mentioned in historic analysis of the inception of the Israeli state is the explicit reference of how British settler colonisation of Ireland features in the establishment of the state of Israel.

When the British Empire sponsored the Zionist movement in Palestine, the British governor of Jerusalem under the mandate, Sir Ronald Storrs, described the creation of Israel serving as a "a little loyal Jewish Ulster" in the Middle East. The powerful political narrative binding the Irish and Palestinians derives from a direct correlation in the occupations and colonial projects both nations were subjected to.

The Irish analogy with Palestine has often been based on the struggle of being a protagonist in another colonial breach with the British Empire. But how strong is Ireland in using its unique position as a small but diplomatically strong country – especially since assuming a seat on the UN Security Council – to hold Israel accountable for its relentless onslaught on the Palestinian people and settler colonialism?

In 2018, Senator Frances Black introduced the Occupied Territories Bill to Seanad Éireann. The bill simply calls for a ban on the importation of goods from illegal settlements in any occupied territories. However, if enacted, the Bill would make Ireland the first country in Europe to end trade with illegal Israeli settlements in the West Bank, on the basis that the settlements violate international humanitarian law and human rights standards and are recognised as being illegal by every country in the world bar Israel. Products from illegal settlements, whether in occupied Palestine or elsewhere, including industrial and agricultural zones, or those natural resources extracted from occupied territories, are the proceeds of international crimes.

Unfortunately. By failing to pass this bill, the Seanad and the Government at the time, made a political decision that Ireland will continue to be a receiver of what is internationally recognised as amounting to stolen goods.

Conclusion

Ireland's diplomatic and marketable politics can lead the way and the chances of a total rethinking of Irish relations with the largest oppressive regimes are higher than they've been in years. Social pressure is a key lever for policy and at the heart of every policy decision lies social context. We have to collectively leverage this and propose compelling arguments for incorporating social context into the design of policy on social justice.

As depressing as Ireland's complicity is in these ongoing 'foreign' injustices, there are reasons to be optimistic, but also to be cautious. Ireland will not confront the interests of the powerful military-industrial complex on its own. Only mobilisation can force them to. The time for such mobilisation is now: the oppressed can wait no longer.

Yara Alagha

Yara is a parliamentary researcher in Seanad Éireann. She also serves as a Board Member for *Amal Association*, a NGO that works with vulnerable women in Ireland including asylum seekers and victims of domestic abuse. She also is a board member of Women for Election, a not-for-profit that seeks to increase female participation in Irish politics. Yara is a Palestinian-Irish social justice activist and works passionately on improving conditions for vulnerable members in Irish society.

Yara recommends:

BOOKS

On Palestine by Ilan Pappé and Noam Chomsky

Justice for Some: Law and the Question of Palestine by Noura Erakat

The Ethnic Cleansing of Palestine by Ilan Pappé

See more of Yara's work:

TWITTER - @arayeire

HIDDEN IN PLAIN SIGHT
A look into Aramark: the profiteering within Direct Provision

Elizabeth Moreton

Have you ever been to Avoca? Isn't it just wonderful? The cakes! Oh, my! And yes, for sure it's a bit pricey but it's such a treat, and such a beacon of Irish culture and business! Brunch for two would be about €40! Sure that's grand, isn't it? And such tasty, fresh, well-cooked food! How about Chopped? Have you ever had one of their epic salads? Such an innovative, healthy and simple idea, and so much choice! Such unreal value! You could totally get lunch every weekday for about €8 per day!

It's great that in Ireland we have the opportunity to spend money on good quality, healthy, nutritionally dense food from home grown companies. How would you feel then, if I told you that your brunch in Avoca, or your weekday salad from Chopped costs more than what one of the most vulnerable people in Ireland is forced to live on each week? Yes, you heard me correctly, one week. In fact, I highly doubt any of us would walk into Avoca with €38.80 and hope to buy a family brunch. Come to think of it, €5.54 wouldn't buy me lunch in Chopped either. €5.54 is the amount an adult in Direct Provision is given to live on per day

€38.80 per week. €5.54 per day.

These Irish businesses are owned by a giant American conglomerate called Aramark; the type of company that denies a mother in Direct Provision a slice of bread for her sick child who had been vomiting for hours? That they serve food so poor in quality and substance, never mind the lack of it, that those forced to eat it would rather starve for fear of becoming unwell unwell; all to expand profit margins.

No choice.
No substance.
No nutritional value.
Culturally inappropriate.
Age inappropriate.
Humanely inappropriate.

Aramark is the largest prison catering company in the USA, with a long history of profiteering from human beings held in captivity. They make billions of dollars each year through their contracts with 500 'correctional facilities' in the US and have a history of neglecting prisoners, serving inedible or non-nutritional foods, or providing a blatant lack of food. In fact, in 2017, Aramark held a revenue of $14.6 Billion (Matterson, 2019) such is their success at making money out of the profiteering of people through willful neglect and abuse. Seemingly the Irish government was so delighted with this résumé that they invited Aramark to our island with open arms to do the same here. Only, this time Aramark aren't profiteering from prisons or penitentiary systems, but from Direct Provision centres. A prison by another name.

Direct Provision is just another 'institution of confinement'.

Another horrific system to add to the long list of Ireland's historic hiding of 'problematic human beings' beyond the periphery of 'regular society'.

Just like the Magdalene Laundries, Mother and Baby Homes, industrial schools, workhouses, and mental health asylums before it, Direct Provision centres are another example of Ireland's historic human rights violations against the most vulnerable in our society. Irish State and society managed to ignore Ireland's system of coercive confinement (O'Sullivan & O'Donnell, 2012); they also continue to claim ignorance about the plight of asylum seekers in Direct Provision.

As Lentin (2020), expresses so accurately, "Ireland's Direct Provision system condemns asylum seekers to a frozen existence, where private for-profit operators such as Aramark, are paid millions to maintain Ireland's version of 'the prison industrial complex'." The housing and accommodation of asylum seekers in Ireland has become a billion-euro industry. Government records, available up to 2018, (nothing since due to an apparent lack of information on where the money is being spent) show that since contracts were signed in 2000, the total amount paid out of the taxpayer's pocket, by our government to companies profiteering from the most vulnerable people on our planet, amounted to approximately €1.2 billion.

These figures account for accommodation alone, not services, facilities management or any of the other expenses associated with running and maintaining one of these detention centres. The actual figure is in fact far higher, but as stated by the RIA, "It is not in the interests of the taxpayer that current details of individual contracts are made known both to the public and to other parties who are, or may be in the future, engaged in negotiations with the RIA."

As of September 2020, Aramark holds private contracts for on-site catering, cleaning and facilities, energy, and property management for three state-owned Direct Provision centres, which accommodate up to 825 asylum seekers. However, this figure has at times been higher, which is a breach of contract.

In 2016, government tender was awarded to Aramark for the Knockalisheen Accommodation Centre in Meelick, which was stated to have a 250-person capacity. It included an estimated pricing schedule for the contract, amounting to a cost of €21.67 per person, per day. According to the tender, the management of this centre, per person, per day, for 365 days per year, would amount to €1.9 million, whilst services provided would equate to €10 million per year. Other fees including insurance would also need to be factored into the operating cost, so actual costs were in fact estimated to be far higher, but at minimum we can assume based on these figures that Aramark would receive in excess of €12 million for their Knockalisheen contract alone that year (Walsh, 2020).

Not only does Aramark own the catering side of Avoca, Chopped and Campbell Bewley Ltd., it is believed that they also now hold an approximate 50% market share of the food services industry in Ireland. It supplies colleges, hospitals and Croke Park stadium to name but a few. It also supplies Direct Provision centres.

Aramark is also extremely popular with the government when awarding any type of property contracts. It manages a rent roll of about €250 million a year and procures supplier services annually of €82 million. Landmark developments managed by Aramark include

Capital Dock in Dublin 4, Beacon South Quarter in Sandyford, the Ilac Centre, Blackrock Shopping Centre, the Irish Life Centre, Cork's English Market and all outsourced IDA industrial estates around Ireland. Aramark Property manages a residential portfolio of m o r e than 5,000 units – including more than 2,000 for Ires Reit – and was recently appointed manager for the Fernbank build-to-rent scheme of 262 high-end apartments in Dublin 14.

All of this wealth, and an unprecedented desire to profit even further with the strong assistance of the Irish Government, by providing the most basic facilities, to human beings who have been forced to leave everything they know behind in fear.

Elizabeth Moreton

"I am a passionate believer in equality and standing up for those who are unable to have their voices heard as clearly as they ought to. The opportunity to contribute to *The Liminal* was an incredible privilege, and one I hope will help highlight how each one of us can make simple choices to not support massive conglomerates like Aramark, who have zero conscience when it comes to human suffering."

MIGRANT WOMEN AND UNDEREMPLOYMENT
A snapshot view of the obstacles facing refugee women in Ireland

Greta Keegan

For the last three years I have been supporting refugee women to prepare for and find work in Ireland. It's hard to think of a more diverse group than those I work with.

They differ in terms of language, culture, religion, ethnicity, nationality, age, political leanings, personality, sexual orientation, gender identity, education, professional experience, and whether they are married or single, whether they have children or not, and if so how many.

In spite of this evident diversity, I can say that the vast majority of women I meet demonstrate incredible resilience, and are eager to begin afresh in Ireland – to earn, to be busy, to work. Yet, we see that many refugee and migrant women are underemployed and face obstacles in accessing employment at a level appropriate to their skills and education. Why is this? An obvious obstacle is language – while there are some excellent English classes run through the Education and Training Boards or community groups, few offer intensive classes or do not cover more advanced levels. This poses difficulties in progressing beyond an intermediate level. While an intermediate level professional placement.

For professionals, foreign qualifications are frequently not recognised, and arduous – if not impossible – registration requirements of professional regulatory bodies (e.g. the Dental Council of Ireland or the Nursing Midwifery Body Ireland) mean that many highly skilled, experienced refugees are blocked from practicing. It also blocks them from availing of upskilling or retraining opportunities to practice their vocation in Ireland.

Protection applicants are faced with paying international student fees for university or PLC courses unless they obtain a scholarship. Compound that with a range of administrative barriers including difficulties with opening bank accounts, applying for driving licences and the near impossibility of securing international police clearance, combined with a lack of documentation or references. All serve to inhibit opportunities.

Childcare is another barrier, with women being more likely to assume the bulk of childrearing duties. This is additionally problematic if one has no family in Ireland, is a single parent or is struggling to make ends meet. Many refugees will have exhausted all financial means upon arriving in Ireland, meaning there is considerable urgency to earn to partake in our consumer society, to become self-sufficient and or to send money to struggling family members abroad – a painful reality for many.

Aside from the personal factors, 'familiarity bias' or indirect discrimination exists in spite of more inclusive recruitment and selection practices. It is saddening to hear anecdotes of a CV with the more familiar name of 'Emma' being selected for interview while the same CV with the more exotic name of 'Sibongubuhle' does not make the cut. These obstacles can also be inter-connected, so one faces the obstacle, for instance of being 'older' and black and a refugee. Refugee women may also self-limit their own ambitions, believing the only roles available to them are as cleaners or carers.

A lack of 'returner', graduate or entry-level positions with on-the-job training is also an issue. Such roles are necessary for the fact that refugees are likely to have a gap in their employment history for reasons connected with their plight or ineligibility to work and their lack of vernacular experience. An absence of a professional network is detrimental in labour market accession, and acquiring one is further complicated by wider patterns of social exclusion. Amid this global health pandemic where online engagement is key, further exclusion can be seen in the form of the digital divide.

On a structural level, international protection applicants with a work permit - called Labour Market Access Permission - are not allowed to work in the public sector, and protection applicants are unable to secure a driving licence for reasons associated with residency status. Barriers connected to a lack of necessary documentation do not necessarily cease upon being recognised as a refugee or being granted subsidiary protection or permission to remain. This is because not having identification documents or sufficient proof of address creates considerable difficulty in opening a bank account, for meeting the HR screening processes of many companies, for obtaining references, or will generally be unable to secure international police clearance if the employers request that this be provided (as for instance, the HSE do). This means that refugees and asylum seekers face particular forms of administrative exclusion, more so than other migrants.

More recently, we have seen positive progression. Black Lives

Matter has been noteworthy in mobilising corporations to critically review their policies and protocols and seek more creative solutions to combat exclusionary mainstream practices. Interest in employee volunteering and CSR (Corporate Social Responsibility) activism has expanded greatly in the midst of the past year's continued lockdown. More people are seeking meaningful engagement and want to make a positive contribution. We have seen more employers who have actively created placements for refugees, in recognition of the particular barriers they face in labour market accession. These measures are encouraging and much-needed.

Positive changes can also be seen in recent changes to the work permit for people in the protection process. This has recently been extended to one day in duration (from 6 months) and protection applicants can apply for this 6 months after applying for asylum in Ireland. This is an encouraging trajectory which will hopefully result in more professional placements.

With greater employer and civic interest and awareness of the issues; with continued advocacy and media interest; with augmented integration, developmental and unemployment supports, hopefully we will see far more employment inclusion in the near future.

Greta Keegan

Greta joined the Irish Refugee Council in March 2018. She initially oversaw a pilot project supporting refugee women to enter the workforce. Having secured continued funding for this work, Greta now coordinates the Integration from Day One women's empowerment programme. Prior to holding this role, Greta assisted people from marginalised backgrounds to enter the workforce. This included recovering addicts, and the long-term unemployed in Ireland and Spain. She holds an M.A. in Social Research from UAB, Barcelona, and a BA in social sciences from Trinity College Dublin.

See more of Greta & the IRC's Work:
    WEBSITE - www.irishrefugeecouncil.ie
    INSTAGRAM - @irishrefugeecouncil
    TWITTER - @IrishRefugeeCo

PREGNANCY AND BABY SUPPORTS

The system of Direct Provision is set up to separate asylum seekers from Irish society. This project is an attempt to create one small crack in the wall.

Louisa Ní Éideáin

There is no official data on how many babies are born into families in Direct Provision. The International Protection Accomodation Service (IPAS), a unit within the Department of Justice & Equality tasked with providing accommodation and ancillary services to asylum seekers, does not collect centralised data on this. The last data from IPAS were published in 2018, with supplemental figures released by the Department of Justice following parliamentary questions. Birth rates are not included in these data. This makes it difficult to estimate the number of families who are in need at any given time. There is a scarcity of statistics at a national level and though I will include some of the data from this particular project, the richness of the Pregnancy and Baby project comes from the stories of all those involved.

Our volunteer group made contact with expectant and recent parents through our network of representatives living in Direct Provision centres around Ireland. We spoke to each parent, usually mothers, to understand their needs and to explain how we hoped to help. The project aimed to provide the basic supplies, clothing, nappies, toiletry products, bedding etc. to expectant families through donated items or those purchased via a fundraising campaign.

A particularly sinister aspect of Direct Provision is the isolation that is deliberately built into the system. Asylum seekers have little control over where they are placed and are often moved between centres around the country, destroying any networks they have in place in a particular location. The system also isolates asylum seekers from Irish society through establishing centres in remote locations. People are provided with limited personal financial resources and different centres have their own rules and norms. This has negative consequences for anyone in the system. During pregnancy these are only heightened.

Imagine fleeing an unsafe home only to arrive to a hostile welcome in a new country, whilst dealing with pregnancy and the Covid-19 restrictions of 2020/2021. This was the prenatal reality for some of the pregnant people we contacted. Others had already spent years in the system of Direct Provision, waiting to understand their longer-term status. This project was also a way of breaking through the boundaries erected by the Direct Provision system, as well as supplying vital materials. It allowed volunteers like me, who have never personally experienced Direct Provision, to build relationships with people living in the system, despite the system's efforts to keep us apart.

It was a Friday afternoon in June 2020, one of the sunny blasts the country received as compensation for the chaos of Covid. I went with another volunteer with bags of supplies to meet a mother outside the Coombe hospital. Her baby had been born prematurely. She had moved across the country to a new Direct Provision centre to be closer to her baby in the Neonatal Intensive Care Unit (still travelling several hours a day to visit), leaving behind the people she had begun to build relationships with at her previous centre. This was childbirth during the time of a pandemic; face-masks, limited visitation and the pervasive fear of infecting the most vulnerable. We handed over bags of tiny premature-sized clothes, nappies and maternity supplies. She would be visiting the hospital daily for another few weeks. We agreed to come back soon with more supplies.

This is not an attempt to tell this woman's story on her behalf, but rather about its impact on me, as an Irish citizen. Seeing the intolerable stress our national policy puts on a person made me fully realise the horrors of Direct Provision and the obligation there is for us to end it. It is through stories and human connections that you can grasp the abstract horror of this system and translate it into the revulsion and anger that lead to action.

Our group collected supplies for over sixty parents and their children over the course of a few months. Baby clothes were washed, dried and packed. Nappies, wipes and creams purchased and dispatched. Volunteers offered the dignity of choice where possible from the assortment of donations we received. We linked in with another network of volunteers, DP Drops, who drive to accommodation centres all over Ireland with supplies and donations. This enabled us to get bulkier donations such as travel systems, pregnancy pillows and cots to the families who needed them.

Through our network of representatives, one living in each Direct Provision centre, we gathered a list of expectant or new parents who were willing to be contacted. We spoke to each person, or to a nominated representative if they did not feel comfortable having the conversation themselves. From here, we made connections and understood their specific needs – did they need breastfeeding or bottle feeding supplies or both? Did they need any maternity items for themselves? Did they have other children who needed essentials? We stayed in touch with the parents with updates on their supplies and with offers of other baby equipment that may have become available. In many cases, babies were born prematurely and we rallied to get premature-sized clothing, nappies and any other supportive items to the mothers as quickly as possible.

Globally, 1 in 10 babies are born prematurely. Severe stress in pregnancy can result in preterm labour. Studies cited by The National Institute for Health and Care Excellence (NICE) estimate that 13% of people experience anxiety during pregnancy, and 12% experience depression. These figures are from a general population, not the specific circumstances of Direct Provision. Unsurprisingly, there is no centralised information available on this topic for asylum seekers in Ireland, nor for their infant mortality rates.

Around 40% of the pregnancies we supported as a volunteer network resulted in preterm deliveries; well above the national average. This was during the Covid-19 lockdown phase between March and June 2020 when initial reports from Limerick Maternity hospitals saw a 73% reduction in preterm births. Some of this was attributed to the reductions in daily stress for pregnant people, as life took on a slower pace and more time was spent at home. This did not apply to people in Direct Provision, many of whom were in centres with known Covid-19 outbreaks and living conditions that did not comply with public health guidance for dealing with a pandemic.

A recent study in the Irish Medical Journal (Murphy et al.), reviewed the outcomes of 81 babies born to 78 asylum seekers in

Ireland between November 2017 and February 2020. The study concluded that infants born to asylum seekers had significantly higher rates (almost double) of NICU admission compared with the general hospital population. The study also highlighted documented use of an interpreter in 20% of cases.

However, sufficient translation services were not always available, leading to miscommunication and difficulties in recording medical histories. Language plays a key role in understanding the supports available within the maternity health care and social care systems in Ireland. A lack of adequate translation services can lead to further isolation, anxiety and misunderstandings for people already in a vulnerable situation.

Another key cohort involved in our project were the donors. Some gave funds online that helped us to purchase nappies, wipes, formula, breastfeeding supplies. Others gave us the clothes and equipment that had been lovingly chosen for their own little ones who were now moving onto bigger things. Parenting books and blogs emphasise the importance of nesting and the final choices made in the weeks before the arrival of a baby.

Nesting options are somewhat limited when you live in one room and receive €38.80 a week as an allowance. People in Direct Provision are denied the opportunity to make many of the tiny decisions that help ease the path into parenthood and allow some sense of control. As volunteers, we offered the dignity of choice where possible. It is a small decency to ask someone if they have a preference between two recently donated prams.

Amongst our donors, there were the parents who parted with

equipment for a much hoped-for second baby that they had accepted was not part of their family's future. They gave their items, hoping that the grief of multiple miscarriages could be soothed knowing that other families were being helped. Other parents had been holding onto clothes and shoes because parting with them meant acknowledging a phase that could never be revisited, for all its exhaustion and tears. Parents arrived who had panic-bought months-worth of Size 0 nappies in their prenatal organisational efforts, only for their baby to outgrow them in days. Parents of babies born early, donated the doll-sized clothes that people had dashed to buy for them in a haze of hospitals and machines, now to be deployed to assist others going through the same trauma.

My home served as one of the drop-off points for donations of buggies, co-sleepers and what seemed at one point, an unending stream of tiny clothes. People would drop bags at the front door and stand back to the gate, respecting social distancing and we would have a quick chat about the project and about what their help meant.

I believe that once you hear the context of life in Direct Provision, you will be moved to take action. These stories are what we have to help texture and closeness to the sparse statistics. Stories of women who gave birth prematurely and then went to nurse the baby living in one room of a B&B, mothering two older children concurrently. The story of the woman who came home with her baby from hospital and the only equipment provided by management in her Direct Provision centre was an old Moses basket without a mattress. The centres are supposed to supply suitable sleep spaces and buggies. Nevertheless, it is often reported to us as not being the case.

We have heard of centre managers refusing donations as 'centre policy,' so that families had not received any community donations for over a year. One woman in Direct Provision told us of the continuous bullying she suffered from a centre manager, with her mattress being seized as a 'punishment,' amongst other incidents. There are also cases of favouritism and alienation, where management single people out and purposely commandeer items from them. There is a reluctance to complain about such treatment as the threat of retaliation has been reportedly issued by some centre management, the implication being that complaining could affect one's asylum application outcome.

Our Pregnancy and Baby Project expanded from being founded and led by one amazing volunteer, to a team of seven across Ireland. We are hoping to start up a family partnership programme through The Danú Project, where we will link families with children of similar ages in a buddy system, to continue the sharing of clothes, toys and other items in a more sustainable way. The volunteer team is looking at ways to digitise the Pregnancy and Baby project catalogue, allowing us to assist people in Direct Provision with the items they need in a more formalised way, giving people as much choice as possible in preparing for their new arrival. We are also exploring ways to partner with Maternity hospitals to ensure we can help people who we may not be already in contact with to access our offerings.

This project owes thanks to many. From the representatives in Direct Provision centres around the county, to people who drove supplies to Monaghan, Mayo, Cork and beyond; the Cuidiú volunteers who offered breast-feeding support despite not being allowed into Direct Provision centres; the parents who washed, folded and dropped off clothing; all of our volunteers; and most of all, the families who let us be part of their experience.

My hope is that this project will not need to exist in the future. The wellbeing of vulnerable parents and babies should not be dependent on informal networks handing over critical supplies in car parks. Babies should not be welcomed home to sleep in unsafe beds, provided by a contractor profiting off contracts from a state who are not fulfilling their international obligations to asylum seekers. For the moment though, we must keep going. We will continue to provide supplies and equipment and support to new parents.

The comment I heard most on my doorstep, from our donors was this: I have wanted to do something to help for ages, I just didn't know how to.

The system of Direct Provision is set up to separate asylum seekers from the communities they live in and from the broader Irish society. This project is an attempt to create one small crack in the wall.

Louisa Ní Éideáin

Louisa works in digital marketing and volunteers with The Danú Project in service to those within the Direct Provision system in Ireland. She is a passionate advocate for women and children's rights, having worked and volunteered with UNICEF and Amnesty International in the past. Having spent most of her adult life as an economic migrant, she feels strongly about the conditions for those who come to live in Ireland seeking asylum or otherwise. Louisa is now head of the maternity kit scheme for The Danú Project.

Louisa Recommends:

ARTICLES

Irish Medical Journal:

https://imj.ie/born-into-direct-provision-outcomes-of-infants-born-to-asylum-seekers/

https://imj.ie/children-growing-up-in-direct-provision/

See more of Louisa's Work:

WEBSITE - danuproject.com

INSTAGRAM - @writerstartingblock / @thedanuproject

TWITTER - @loulylady

CREATING A NETWORK OF SUPPORT DURING A TIME OF ISOLATION
How social media became a vehicle for aid and connected the public with people in Direct Provision.

Louisamay Hanrahan

My mom met a friend of mine and he told us of a life growing up in a caravan in Meath. I had heard rumblings of Direct Provision ,but I was unclear as to what it was and what people experienced going through it. After hearing about my friend's experience, I took to the internet and started trying to find out all about the Direct Provision system online.

On March 1st 2020, I decided to take a deeper look into Covid-19. I'd been hearing word of it being 'just a cold' but after seeing a tweet detailing it ravaging Italy and hearing reports that it was taking over the south of Spain I became more curious. Twitter revealed to me a world of lockdowns, crammed hospitals, fear and an undeniable threat of Covid-19 ravaging across Ireland. After seeing a tweet from an Irish doctor calling out for volunteers to help medical staff I started an instagram group called *@coronavirusvolunteersdublin*. The aim of the group was to get volunteers together to help out with whatever was needed during the Covid pandemic.

As I reached over 1,000 followers on this Instagram, I realised it had the ability to spread awareness and mobilize volunteers. We spread information about locking down the pubs, feeding the heroes, getting masks to nursing homes and more. The group was followed by big influencers who shared our findings to their followers, helping us get help to those in need.

I studied Human Health and Disease at Trinity College Dublin. This armed me with the ability to understand Covid-19, how it spread and how to identify communities that were at higher risk of it spreading among them. I thought a lot about the Direct Provision centres and how people were in close quarters, without the ability to social distance.

On March 30th, an asylum seeker wrote to us asking for help. "We urgently need gloves, masks, hand sanitizer, hand soap and bleach," they said. I was not surprised, and was eager to do what I could in order to get them the necessary tools required to slow down the spread of Covid-19.

There was one big problem; we were in the two-kilometre lockdown phase. I posted the request for help to my group of volunteers and realised getting asylum seekers the help they needed was going to be complicated. Previously I'd been relying on people to deliver goods to hospitals, nursing homes or to whomever was looking for help. As Ireland was in lockdown and there were over 300 people in this centre in need of hygiene products, I realised getting them what they needed was going to be no easy feat. After a couple of days thinking it through, I set up a GoFundMe.

Within a day, €1,000 was raised and I set off purchasing soap and bleach in bulk. As it wasn't permitted to buy hygiene products in bulk from local stores due to supply shortages, I rang every wholesaler in Dublin. I purchased soap from Musgrave only to turn up the next day and find out they'd sold it on by accident and were sold out. Eventually I found Selco out in the Wicklow mountains and I purchased enough soap and bleach for the whole centre. People online were starting to rally around me and support other centres. Easter eggs were dropped to many centres in Dublin. Kind Bars donated over €5,000 worth of products, and there was much more.

I had €400 left from the GoFundMe so decided to help another centre. I rang organisations that had been helping Direct Provision for a long time and got reliable contacts for centres in need of hygiene products. Followers on the Instagram account kept donating to allow me to help another centre, and then another. They then started offering help with physical donations. It was still very difficult to purchase all the supplies in bulk; every wholesaler in or near Dublin had no soap to their name.

The travel restrictions were still strict in Dublin, and we weren't allowed to have group gatherings, so I couldn't organise a way for people to drop supplies to me. To solve this, I started to drive around Dublin in my little Nissan Micra (The 'NisVan') and pick up hygiene supplies that followers had bought to donate to Direct Provision.

"Another day, another Direct Provision Drop." I filmed these drop offs on my iPhone and posted them to Instagram to raise awareness so we could continue helping centres. As I got to know people within these centres, I discovered more about the horrific reality they are living in.

"Toothpaste in our centre is 6 euro."

"We have to go hungry to purchase hygiene supplies." My followers reacted strongly as I shared my learnings with them and started to donate more than hygiene products (shoes, nappies, food, clothes etc). I'd bring them to a centre and I soon realised people within the centres were delighted with whatever we could bring them.

After college, I worked in growing early stage startups. I launched Deliveroo in Ireland, and was involved in early days of Patreon & the Web Summit. Using the knowledge on how to grow early stage companies, I put together a plan to raise awareness for DP and grow the GoFundMe so I could continue helping centres in the long term. However, I didn't actually get to put my marketing plan into action as it all took off right before that!

On May 31st 2020, I interviewed my friend Katja (@katja_miaa) on Instagram live. It was the day before the Black Lives Matter protests took place in Ireland. We discussed racism in Ireland and highlighted to our followers that it's not just a problem experienced in America. We discussed her experiences of growing up as a black woman in Ireland and highlighted Direct Provision. This amassed over 16k views within a day.

On Blackout Tuesday I posted about the GoFundMe on my instagram page. My followers immediately supported it and the GoFundMe got shared to over 5,000 people's stories. We raised over €40,000 in 2 days, from over 2,800 people.

What happened after this still blows my mind. Other people started up pages all over Ireland to get donations to centres near them. I changed the name of my Instagram to *@letshelpdirectprovision*, and helped people set up their own pages under the name of *@dpdrops*. Other groups started up as well like *@dpdonations*.

All of a sudden, centres all over Ireland were being brought hygiene products, laptops, bikes, food, clothes and more. Volunteers started coming with me on drops and helping me distribute donations to the centres. In one month we distributed €100,000 worth of donations!

Businesses began to reach out to me to help. I received over €100k worth of toothpaste from Spotlight Oral Care; 1,000 hand sanitizers from The Handmade Soap Company; all the clothes I needed for centres from Nine Crows; €5,000 worth of soap & moisturizer from Lush; Coffee from Moyee Coffee and so much more. Our followers dropped 1000's of euros worth of baby supplies to us to give to new mothers in Direct Provision.

We had brave people from Direct Provision write in to tell their stories. Graphic designers in Dublin helped illustrate these stories on Instagram. The Irish community banded together to support and grow *@letshelpdirectprovision*, and to show people in Direct Provision that they care and they want change.

Louisamay Hanrahan

Louisamay founded *Let's Help Direct Provision*, an organisation that allows you to donate products directly to people living in DP. Louisamay comes from a startup background, she was involved with launching Deliveroo in Ireland and helping grow Patreon & Websummit. Alongside running *Let's Help* she is also the founder of @supstartupagency where she helps startups start up.

Louisamay is passionate about improving the day to day life of asylum seekers. She aims to keep improving getting donations to those in DP & helping spread awareness through educational content posted on the @*letshelpdirectprovision* Instagram & *letshelpdirectprovision.com* website.

Louisamay Recommends:

PODCAST & MEDIA

Lets Help Podcast

Irish Refugee Council Reports

The Black and Irish Podcast

See more of Louisamay's Work:

INSTAGRAM - @letshelpdirectprovision / @louisamayh / @supstartupagency

WEBSITE - letshelpdirectprovision.com / supstartupagency.com

MENTAL HEALTH ON THE MARGINS

Trauma paints a direct line to mental illness, which needs to be taken seriously.

Blessing Dada

I want to open this with a small mention of the P word.

Privilege is not always just about race or gender, but is a series of interrelated hierarchies and power dynamics that touch all facets of social life. Race, class, gender, sexual orientation, religion, education, gender identity and physical ability are just some examples.

In the case of Direct Provision, racial privilege plays a big part. It is usually equated with white privilege since power, money and influence tend to be concentrated among caucasians in Western Europe and North America. A personal privilege I can recognise, is that my family was in Ireland before the abhorrent system of Direct Provision came into place. I was born with automatic entitlement to citizenship, without depending on the nationality or residential history of my parents before the 1st of January 2005. With this, I was able to live normally: allowing me to vote, work and more.

I'm a black mental health advocate with a passion for social justice issues and have openly lived experiences. I wanted to use my privileges to voice the importance of diversity and inclusion in an ever- evolving and beautifully diverse Ireland. The experience of asylum seekers is unique and requires specialised intervention and services.

Mental Health

This is to bring awareness to the unique struggles that under-represented groups face in regard to mental illness. 'Minority' can be associated with racial, ethnic, or cultural groups. It also now expands to a wide range of marginalised and underserved communities, including refugee, immigrant and religious groups. Our identities are formed not only by what we believe to be true, but also by the views of those around us.

In many ways, specific communities (oftentimes referred to as marginalised; people of colour; minority) are seen as victims or broken. As a community, they must constantly work towards combatting those stereotypes to maintain wellbeing. It is at the intersection of all these nuanced identities where one must constantly confront the biases and stereotypes used by others to define them. What I see in the people in Direct Provision is strength. Courage. They are warriors.

People from various cultures can have a different perspective and interpretation of the term 'mental health'. It is well-known that other ethnic communities may not share Western conceptualisation or use Western language around mental health.

I speak from my own experience, perspective, and knowledge as an Afro-Irish. In the African community, family, community, and spiritual beliefs tend to be great sources of strength and support. This has a tendency to lead people to rely on faith, family, and social communities rather than turning to healthcare professionals, even when medical or therapeutic treatment may be necessary.

Mental health issues don't discriminate, but the current system does. We must not leave Direct Provision out of our activism. We shall not. The mental well-being of all people is essential to the well-being of our society and our country. It is a key foundation that appears to be highly underestimated. What about those still waiting for the processing of their papers?

Direct Provision was originally introduced as an emergency measure in 1999, yet here we still are. Over twenty years of an abhorrent system which inflicts State-sanctioned harm upon vulnerable people who have come to Ireland seeking sanctuary. Before 2000, asylum seekers were catered for within the traditional welfare state and entitlement was based on need, just like the average Irish citizen.

The current system is inhumane and degrading. Asylum seekers deserve the same human rights as anyone else. To anyone reading this: let's not continue to marginalise them further by getting informed and equipped with tools. They are made to feel invisible and are excluded from society. The process of separation and exclusion leads to Othering, and creates a 'them' and 'us'. Please, put yourself in their shoes and think how you would feel if it were you and your family.

Multiple factors determine mental health outcomes. The more risk factors people are exposed to, the greater the potential impact on their mental health. Some of these factors include:

- Having a parent who has had mental health problems;
- Social exclusion;
- Loss of extended family and that of their significant social Networks;

- Long periods of time spent in an institutional setting;
- Stress associated with the asylum process and uncertainty surrounding their status;
- Lack of employment possibilities;
- Cultural shock;
- Lack of cohesive social support;
- Living in poverty or being homeless;
- Experiencing discrimination, perhaps because of their race, sexuality, or religion;
- And many more.

It is vital to acknowledge that the mental health requirements of refugees, migrants and asylum seekers can differ greatly within those groups as well as from that of the general population. It is likely that their needs cannot be adequately addressed by generic mental health services, without additional expertise, training and funding.

While mainstream mental-health supports are in principle available to asylum seekers, many direct-provision residents may be unaware, or unable to access, such services. Many of those seeking asylum have witnessed war, atrocities, persecution, natural disasters and grinding poverty, leaving many with complex psychological needs that can only be addressed by easily accessible and culturally sensitive services.

IMPACT OF MENTAL HEALTH ON CHILDREN AND YOUNG PEOPLE

The emotional wellbeing of children and young people is just as important as their physical health overall. However, the experience of those in Direct Provision is unique and requires specialised services and intervention. For the most part, things that happen to children and young people don't lead to mental health problems on their own, but traumatic events can trigger problems for those who are already vulnerable.

According to *Doras* (an independent, non-profit, NGO working to promote and protect the rights of people from a migrant backgrounds in Ireland), about 30% of people in Direct Provision are kids, that's over 1,700 children.

Failure to deal with mental health pressures, such as growing up in an unsuitable environments which harm milestone developments, can result in serious problems for these children in the future. Direct Provision is a system which is little more than state-sponsored poverty. Families and individuals (totaling more than 7,000 people across Ireland) are forced to live in cramped communal conditions. Most parents and young adults are unable to work, as the majority of people who live in Direct Provision centres have no right to access employment.

I have read stories on Instagram of how adolescent and young adults were deeply affected and isolated by government policy, which did not allow them to further their education or seek employment. The pain of seeing classmates and friends continuing education while they couldn't has been seen to affect their mental health. Children and young people need and have the right to live in an environment that fully supports encourages them to reach their full emotional and developmental potential.

When it comes to the current Covid-19 environment, the issues are amplified. With parents unable to seek employment, and only €38.60 a week in government support, there are little to no extra funds left for educational items. Schoolbooks, computers, internet access, tablets, or phones for the children to continue their studies remotely become inaccessible.

The state did not make extra provisions for the children living in Direct Provision during the Covid-19 pandemic, despite the online learning that was implemented by all educational institutions. Without internet access and online-capable hardware such as tablets or laptops, these young people lost months of mandatory education. Every child deserves an education as their shining hope for a better life in the future. It also provides much-needed normalcy and structure while living in the poor conditions of Direct Provision. Organisations and advocates rallied together in order to raise funds and donation drives for for tablets, laptops, internet modems or subscriptions to provide students with fair access to education.

There is an Irish seanfhocal (saying) that says, *mol an óige agus tiocfidh sí*. It means 'praise the youth and it will prosper'. If this government truly cares about the future of this country, it will take the necessary steps to support and invest in the well-being of its young people. We need long-term governmental actions and support, as we cannot continue to only rely on the generosity of people advocating.

As a country, with such significant history of harm done to children in institutional care, it is disheartening to see history repeat itself. People have united to condemn the Mother and Baby Homes, and the concept of institutionalising vulnerable people. Will they now commit to end Direct Provision?

IMPACT OF MENTAL HEALTH ON ADULTS

The ability of asylum seekers to overcome often traumatic experiences and deal with multiple losses they have experienced, is unlikely to be reduced if their environment remains traumatic. This is coming from the heart-breaking stories I've heard during the rise of Black Lives Matter awareness, where testimonies were shared to advocating pages. We hear too many stories of people who feel they have been abandoned, with nowhere to turn to for mental-health support.

Adult asylum seekers are more likely to experience mental illness than refugees and Irish citizens because of disproportionate exposure to post-migration stressors. These stressors can include insecure residency and obstacles in obtaining the right to work

I have read testimonies of parents who are forced to live in communal settings with a range of other adults and children. They usually have no previous connections to one another. Parents who feel like they are not doing their best nor being a positive example to their kids and are unable to seek employment. They survive on only €38.60 per week in government support. There are stories of gaslighting and managerial abuses of power. Asylum seekers feel they cannot challenge them out of fear of being punished.

Unsuitable accommodation; delays in case processing; substance misuse and addiction; a lack of support services; the impact of Covid-19. These are all detrimentally affecting the mental health of people in Direct Provision. It is necessary for staff and management of centres to be able to appropriately respond to the mental health needs of residents, including people at high risk of suicide.

Arif from Afghanistan was the second asylum seeker to have died by suicide in Direct Provision in less than 5 months, after a previous passing in April 2020. Arif was placed in a small, dark room during isolation at Tracey's Hotel in Co. Monaghan in early August 2020. This triggered negative responses to the traumatic experiences of his journey to Ireland. Some of the residents at the centre saw him walking around the centre at am the morning before his death. Arif had emailed IPAS requesting to leave the centre many times.

Seeing and hearing tragic stories like that, in unprecedented times, sparked people to start up petitions, make phone calls and send emails to Ministers Helen Mc Entee and Roderic O'Gorman. They demanded investigations into this matter and to cancel the contract of Trenthall Ltd for human rights abuses since 2018.

This should not have happened in the first place. When we advocate for mental health awareness, we advocate for *all*.

Death in a Direct Provision centre is deeply traumatic because being stripped of personal autonomy, the right to privacy and the dignity that comes with it does not help in processing that trauma, even if a person goes through the HSE's mental health supports services. In many cases, they are prescribed sleeping pills or antidepressants which do not help process trauma but numb it instead. This also doesn't deal with the fact Direct Provision has its own traumas that further compound pre-migration trauma.

PANDEMIC

With outbreaks in places such as Monaghan, Kildare, Laois, and Offaly, some of the people affected in those areas also unfortunately experienced poor physical health due to Coronavirus. I criticise the state for failing to initially consider Direct Provision's needs, especially in Covid-19 response, considering they were aware that residents continue to share bedrooms and communal facilities. Asylum seekers don't have opportunities to socially distance or effectively self-isolate. The impact of Covid-19 on the lives of those in Direct Provision, including increased levels of isolation and the stigma associated with being an asylum seeker, is very concerning.

There will likely be more residents expressing suicidal ideation during this Covid-19 pandemic and future crises if the government don't respond with necessary aid. Accessible supports are also required for those suffering from substance misuse and addiction arising from forced idleness, including social exclusion, long-term unemployment and trauma.

Owodunni "Ola" Mustapha

Ola is someone who is such a driving force and inspiration to me and so many others. Ola and I have two things in common: we're both Nigerian and have both experienced domestic violence. She is a mum of three, who has resided at the Direct Provision centre in Ballyhaunis, County Mayo for five years. She had to flee to Ireland because of domestic violence. I fell into homelessness due to domestic violence last year and got out just a few days before starting college. In my worst moments, it was Ola that I kept in the back of my mind to drive self-motivation. If she could do it; then so could I.

She became a vocal force of inspiration for her community. She committed to building herself and her community up to ensure human and civil rights to all. She quickly became a leading volunteer at her local asylum seeker centre and continues to be the change that she wants to see, to help others rise in her community and throughout

Ireland.

She is also a double nomination winner: 1st for winning the prestigious Christine Buckley Volunteer of the Year award in 2019 (rightly so) and that was a huge achievement for her. Then, in 2020 with her project Ballyhaunis Inclusion Project she won the Volunteer of the Year award in the Small Groups category.

I used to watch out for her Facebook videos of her lived experiences in the system, with a series called, Diary of an Asylum Seeker, a personal blog of a woman who arrived in Ireland over years ago with bags of hope and shed-load of dreams. However, her reality has been a nightmare as she's stuck in limbo and facing uncertainty about the future.

Oh, how I hope she knows how powerful her tongue is. This woman has been through hell and back and I applaud her for still fighting for herself and her children's lives. As Ola says, "Behind every number ID, there are real people whose lives are impacted by this endless wait in DP." She expresses and vocalises her thoughts frequently on Twitter, which makes it all the more real. Many people become so used to hearing these types of stories and don't think that it is so close to home. There is power in hearing from those of lived experiences and I hope she knows how much she is valued with all of the hard work that she contributes to.

Ola is also a major link between asylum seekers at her shelter and valuable refugee policy information that Mayo Intercultural Action provides. She keeps individuals updated on the evolving policy that refugees must know on, despite having her own issues. Because of selfless advocates like Ola, perceptions of refugees are slowly improving across her community and if you see this I hope I have put these in the best words possible: thank you so much for all that you do. You're an inspiration

In conclusion, I want us all to take part in moving toward change and equal opportunities. Informing, educating and accepting that we do not know all that we need to about each other's culture is the first step, and it's important we care enough to ask questions with cultural humility. Anyone can experience the challenges of mental illness, regardless of their background. However, background and identity can make access to mental health treatment much more difficult

The key message is not to be silent. It's not enough to be not racist. You have to be actively anti-racist in order to see progression. Change. Be on the right side of Irish history. "Listen to marginalised voices," is all well and good until marginalised people disagree with each other and you actually have to do the reading. Don't thrive on other people's oppression and suffering. We're in this together. Be the change you want to see in society, to the best of your own abilities.

Blessing Dada

"I hope this piece will help us all on the road to raising awareness and instigating conversations on the trend of institutionalism in Ireland. I hope it helps on the journey to abolishing the current system of Direct Provision from a mental health perspective. With the current government in place, and the rise of vocalised change with the Black Lives Matters movement; there's no better time to saturate everyone's awareness now and going forward for all things future politics, to inform each other enough to help make informative and necessary changes. Mental health matters."

Blessing Recommends:

BOOKS

What a Time to be Alone by Chidera Eggerue

The Unapologetic Guide to Black Mental Health by Rheeda Walker

See more of Blessing's Work:

INSTAGRAM - @blezzingdada

FACEBOOK - @Blezzung Dada

LINKEDIN - Blessing Dada

No Play
The mental health effects of Direct Provision on children

Aoife Mary Smith

For many children in Direct Provision, their experience is a challenging and psychologically demanding one. It has been long established that children living within the Direct Provision system in Ireland commonly experience income poverty, material deprivation, housing deprivation and social exclusion (Fanning & Veale, 2004). However, this is just a short list of the difficulties that they face. The continuous decline or removal of play areas and opportunities for play, coupled with the severely traumatic circumstances experienced by some children within Direct Provision, could have catastrophic effects on their mental health, even into adulthood.

The Declaration of the Rights of the Child (United Nations, 1959) explicitly states that every child has the right to play. The Oxford English Dictionary (2020) defines play as 'The engagement in activity for enjoyment and recreation rather than a serious or practical purpose.' The United Nations insist that play is one of several essential development rights within the life of a child, along with survival rights and protection rights (United Nations, 1959; Children's Rights, 2020).

However, studies carried out in the UK reveal that the amount of by about 90% since the 1970s due to societal and perceived safety changes (Whitebread, 2017). Closer to home, a study conducted in Ireland by O'Connor et. al (2017) revealed that just under two fifths of surveyed children played outside in wild areas/nature.

Asylum-seeking children have stricter limitations in comparison, as they must also deal with the constant restriction of autonomy, agency and freedom due to the removal of play areas and restricted movements within Direct Provision centres. Not only does the Direct Provision system candidly oppose the survival rights of asylum-seeking children by providing inadequate living standards, this system consistently removes the key development right of play from children who are already suffering, which dangerously hinders key elements of their cognitive development (Karlsson, 2018).

Play is a significant component of healthy development. It is pleasurable, spontaneous, and rewarding. Play can be categorised in numerous ways, however The National Institute for Play (2020) divides the types of play into seven categories: Attunement or mimic play, body play and movement, object play, social play, imaginative and pretend play, storytelling/narrative play and creative play.

Each type of play supports the exploration of various experiences and potential real-life consequences, encouraging the development of well-rounded and competent adults, and studies suggest that vigorous play as a child is paramount in becoming a mature and loving adult (Eriksson, 1977; Nijhof et. al, 2018; Erickson, 1985).

Jean Piaget (1962) speculated that make-believe play in particular creates opportunities for the imitation of real-life conflicts; the shaping of ideal resolutions, thus allows for the processing and alleviation of negative emotions. Narratives and storytelling support the presence of a wide variety of positive and negative experiences and provide ample time to negotiate these experiences within oneself or with others in a non-structured and psychologically spacious way. Collaboration when creating narratives and telling stories has also been linked to clear identity development, which is a staple part of positive mental health (Seja & Russ, 1999).

Additionally, play is a significant contributor to healthy emotional development. Emotional understanding is 'the process by which people make inferences about their own and others' feelings and behaviours that in turn influence their thoughts and actions' (Nannis, 1988; Seja & Russ, 1999). Understanding emotions is important, as this allows children to become skilled at redirecting and controlling displays of emotion and emotional experiences.

A child's comprehension of emotions results in a more accurate estimation of how different circumstances and outcomes may affect their emotional state. It also encourages accurate interpretations of and reactions to other people's emotional presentations. Along with this, creativity and problem solving either alone or with others are vital qualities that are explored and improved upon with play. In fact, simply playing with Lego™ is linked to the improvement of mathematical skills (Christie & Johnsen, 1983; Nath & Szücs, 2014).

The complex cognitive processes that take place during play ultimately lead to high quality relationships, a smoother social acceptance process and an increased likelihood for positive social integration (Creasey et. al 1998).

Furthermore, play acts as an outlet for the expression of strong emotions such as frustration and rage, which allows the child to cope with environmental challenges and, in turn, promotes positive mental health (Sutton-Smith, 2008). Unfortunately, however, play is extremely limited in Direct Provision centres, making these vital cognitive processes almost impossible to encourage within developing children. Interrupted, inhibited or hindered cognitive development could have devastating effects on a child's mental health. In addition to the absence of essential play opportunities, extremely traumatic events have negatively impacted the mental health of many children living within Direct Provision centres.

Aside from any severe stressors encountered prior to coming to Ireland, some children have had near-death experiences and others have witnessed death while living within the Direct Provision system. Some have even witnessed a recent hunger strike at the Skellig Star Direct Provision Centre in Cahersiveen, County Kerry, as a result of the Irish Government's refusal to listen to a group of people who have been waiting too long to be heard. Research shows that adverse childhood experiences such as these regularly can translate into mental health issues in later years (Karatekin, 2018).

From a biological perspective, stress and trauma weaken a vital brain structure known as the amygdala. Amygdala damage is associated with issues such as irregular or abnormal emotional expression and attention difficulties, as well as a host of other cognitive problems which are linked to the development of mental health difficulties (Park et. al, 2018). Asylum seekers experience unique stressors aside from the trauma that Ireland's Direct Provision centres cause.

A study by Wilson et. al (2013) revealed that 71.9% of forced migrant participants had family members or friends who had been murdered, 65.6% had experienced a lack of food or water, and 53.1%

had experienced physical beatings. All of these harrowing events occurred prior to migration. When an asylum seeker does finally arrive in a new country, resettlement stress (triggered by the loss of a homeland, friends, family and possessions) can contribute to anxiety and depression diagnoses. The difficulties involved in potentially learning a new language and assimilating into a new culture adds to this psychological pressure.

Furthermore, asylum seekers are forced to cope with uncertain circumstances and constantly live with the worry of deportation while the addition of bleak post-migration living conditions, such as the living conditions within Ireland's Direct Provision centres, put asylum seekers at an even greater risk of poor mental health.

Many studies report high rates of psychological distress and disorders such as anxiety, depression and post-traumatic stress disorder (PTSD) among asylum seekers and their children.

On some occasions, current traumatic circumstances can be associated with previous traumatic experiences, which encourages the persistence of PTSD and other psychiatric symptoms (Silove et. al, 2000). PTSD is associated with debilitating symptoms such as hyper-vigilance, avoidance behaviour, intrusive thoughts, nausea, flashbacks, insomnia, and dissociative amnesia (McVane, 2020). It is usually diagnosed when a person has experienced one or more traumatic events. Asylum seekers are even more vulnerable to PTSD when compared to refugees (Silove et. al, 2000; Crumlish et. al, 2011), with the PTSD risk factors including insecure accommodation, excessively stringent asylum processes, and difficulties dealing with immigration.

Children of asylum seekers are at risk of developing mental health problems alongside their parents (Ryan et. al, 2009). Parental wellbeing plays a vital role in the adequate mental health care of children who find themselves in asylum-seeking circumstances, as it has been established that children feel displacement stress via observing their distressed parents, who seem to be approximately five times more likely to be diagnosed with a psychiatric illness when compared to Irish citizens (McMahon et. al, 2007).

International research also suggests that asylum-seeking children are more commonly diagnosed with psychiatric disorders in comparison to children who are citizens of their country of residence, and unaccompanied asylum-seeking children are at an even higher risk of mental illness diagnoses (Pinto et. al, 2007; Sanchez-Cao et. al, 2013). Despite the ongoing discussions surrounding the adverse effects of Ireland's Direct Provision system on asylum seeker mental health, Ireland's asylum-seeking children and their parents commonly face distress that compromises their wellbeing.

Ireland is witnessing a devastating pandemic that is claiming loved ones, and her economy is bruised. People in Ireland are facing unprecedented stressors that affect life from every angle. Asylum seekers have both unique and additional stressors that compromise their mental health aside from Covid-19's drastic effects. While adult asylum seekers possess little autonomy, asylum-seeking children find themselves in an even more restricted and compromised position.

The removal of play takes away a vital channel for expression, emotional growth, cognitive development, and social progression. The addition of traumatic circumstances and events invites debilitating psychological symptoms and disorders. The Irish Government has been willing to risk the mental wellbeing of asylum-seeking children for the past twenty years, and this needs to stop. When the next generation asks what was done about this, is the answer really going to be 'nothing'?

Ireland's history is steeped in rebellion, camaraderie, and fighting for justice. Asylum seekers and asylum-seeking children deserve better care. Therefore, Ireland has an obligation to remember who she is and what she stands for, as no child deserves to suffer at the hands of a system that is supposed to protect them from such psychological harm.

Aoife Mary Smith

When Aoife was fascinated by an elective Psychology module that she completed in her final year of her BSc. Veterinary Nursing degree, she knew that this was the realm that she would thrive in. After a few years of acting school, life experience, and living in Australia, she qualified as a psychologist in June 2020. Aoife passionately believes that as a psychologist, and as a psychotherapist in training, it is her job to educate herself on everybody's story so that she can care for others to the best of her ability. When she isn't supporting Ireland's Veterinary community on Instagram, she has the pleasure of working on essential projects such as *The Liminal*.

See more of Aoife's Work:
    INSTAGRAM - @athenasmindveterinary

DIVERSITY, INCLUSION AND INTEGRATION IN IRISH UNIVERSITIES
Integration needs to be prioritised in Irish Universities.

Paula Martinez

I recently organised and hosted a panel discussion on decolonisation and education in Ireland. It was an incredible opportunity to hear what Black and migrant students at University College Dublin (UCD), Trinity College Dublin and the University of Limerick (UL) thought about the topic. The panel discussion was part of a Diversity Week I organised for UCD, as I was elected the first Diversity and Inclusion officer for the Student's Union (SU).

The fact I am the first person to occupy this role already says a lot on the subject of decolonising Irish educational institutions. Even though it is considered a Global University, UCD only created an Equality and Diversity Group (EDI) this year, and it is also the first year the SU has a Diversity and Inclusion officer.

The topics of racism, xenophobia and decolonisation seem foreign to many Irish people. They are often brushed aside by someone saying, "Irish people are the ones that suffered, not the ones creating suffering." This mentality makes it very difficult to talk about and explore solutions to these topics. As an initial reaction, we are often faced with rejection and gaslighting.

On a broader scale, the disbelief surrounding these issues became apparent through the surprise and shock white Irish people expressed at the sudden surge in race discussions in May 2020. Again and again, on social media and other media outlets people said, "That is an American problem." However, this received strong backlash from the Black Irish and migrant communities who had to open up about personal experiences in order to outline the racism that takes place in Ireland. Discussion also began to gain traction around the Direct Provision system.

The belief that Ireland has no role on the other side of the story of colonisation or discrimination, because of their colonised past, has worked in favor of the government. It has created an illusion that the country and governors are not really the ones keeping people in Direct Provision.

The government exploits international students as money bags, rather than viewing them as assets to the educational sphere. They also turn a blind eye to any possible educational or cultural integration plans for immigrants who came and work in jobs Irish people did not want to do anymore.

It is very easy for Irish people to completely negate their part in the exploitation of people and negate their white privilege due to their colonial past. But this does not make it right nor does it erase how many people are treated as second-class citizens by the Irish State.

I am a Brazilian-Ecuadorian migrant living in Ireland, it also happens that I am part of the African diaspora. I have studied for five years in Dublin. I completed my undergraduate degree here, and now I am finishing my master's degree in Racial Issues, Decolonisation and Migration Law.

I ran for Diversity and Inclusion officer because I strongly believe education is a powerful preventative tool against racism and xenophobia. In my four years of undergraduate studies, in a highly marketed Global University, I realised what a colonial education was, and what it did to my peers. I'm speaking mostly about the ones that did not get the chance to study abroad, travel much or meet people from other countries.

My father was a diplomat and I've had the fortune and privilege to travel all around the world since I was five years old. This meant I could attend top international schools full of students from everywhere. I have, since an early age, a very in-depth knowledge in politics, economy and diplomacy, as well as migration issues due to my dad's teachings.

My goal is to have many events, seminars, talks, groups, book clubs, sport events and just general spaces created to promote and encourage inclusion. Every European country has a long way to go to tackle racism and xenophobia, but having lived in France and Spain and done studies on Germany and The Netherlands, at least countries in continental Europe accept their part on colonialism and promoting white supremacy. At least by accepting it, these countries do promote and facilitate cultural and integration events for its young population as well as having a wider acceptance of refugees (ex: right to work for refugees and how a French judge had to push it to Ireland and still is pretty bad).

There is a lot of work to do everywhere in the world about these topics. Racism and xenophobia emerge as very different issues depending on their context within each country. There is not one easy fix. To me, a big problem in Ireland is its inability to accept that it's part of being a white western power in the world.

Ireland has thrived in the world. A big part of this comes from whiteness and the other to its geographical position. This does not mean Ireland isn't a land of hard working people, or that they did not go through a lot, but we have to understand its privilege. Other countries could not progress as Ireland has, even though they have had similar stories of migration.

What supported Ireland to become the power that it is now is its American ally (one of the most powerful countries on earth), which fell in love with claiming roots from this remote white heritage. We must also remember that everyone who benefits from privilege, passively or otherwise, contributes to the marginalisation and discrimination of other groups. This is why anti-bigotry work is so important.

From the very good read *How the Irish Became White* by Noel Ignatiev, PhD Art Mcdonald, writes, "It's a sympathetic yet tragic story of how race has been a defining characteristic in U.S. culture and how the race question has also plagued the white working class in this country. One might say that it is a story of how the Irish exchanged their greenness for whiteness, and collaborated with the dominant white culture to continue the oppression of African Americans."

The outlook Irish people tend to have on their historical suffering does not allow us to have open conversations and look for solutions to racism and xenophobia in Ireland. This often comes from the mix up between slavery and indentured servitude. "White men in America and elsewhere...say, we were enslaved too, […] Irish indentured slavery saw Irish people serving periods of seven years of labour in the Caribbean and British North America in what is known as indentured slavery. After a period of seven years, they were freed, unlike African slaves whose children, and their children were born into slavery," said Anthea Butler, Associate Professor of Religious Studies and Africana Studies, and the History of Slavery University of Pennsylvania, when she delivered the 2019 Annual Humanities Horizons Lecture at Trinity College Dublin in 2019.

All the study and projects I work on are based on researching and analysing other successful cases of economic and social integration in different countries (New Zealand, Brazil, Canada, The Netherlands, Belgium) and to see how they can be applied to the Irish context. This country is my home now, and I believe education is the answer to a fairer, more hospitable and integrated Ireland.

BiaFriend Q&A
With Zee, Caroline McCarthy and Grace McCarthy. Chaired by Fiadh Melina

I sat down virtually with BiaFriend organisers Caroline and Grace on a Sunday night in February. Their project had taken off the month before, with staggering positive response.

We laughed as we wished each other a Happy Valentine's Day and mused over the absurdity of how many hours we now spend on Zoom. Zee joined us shortly after and gave us the chance to bid a whirlwind "Hello!" to her gorgeous kids.

BiaFriend provides asylum seekers, migrants and refugees with a platform to teach cooking classes online. The classes are there to share culture, heritage and joy through their favourite recipes. Booking fees cover the cost of the teaching cook's ingredients and any surplus from the first round was donated to The Danú Project. It's a simple yet incredibly intimate and effective project which has brought a smile to so many faces.

In early February, I was fortunate enough to sit in on one of Zee's sessions in preparation for this Q&A. The atmosphere throughout the class was light and welcoming. Attendees got the chance to introduce themselves between soaking couscous and chopping vegetables. Towards the end of the class, a chorus of appeased voices flooded through my screen as the cooks unmuted themselves and shared their excitement. We couldn't smell the aromas in each other's kitchens, but the collective experience was still fantastic in its own Zoom-esque way.

FIADH: Food was a frequent subject that came up in the Winter zoom chat rooms. Could you tell me a little bit about how BiaFriend grew from that? And what is your own background in food?

CAROLINE: I've worked in the food sector for over five years. Pre-pandemic, I was teaching digital skills to Syrian refugees with the Refugee Council in London. As well as that, I was helping another charity called Breadwinners, which supports young asylum seekers in London. Before that, I was working on a charity that no longer exists, called *Homes for Syrians*.

When I moved back to Ireland, I became involved in virtual lockdown chat rooms with asylum seekers. I hadn't actually known a lot about Direct Provision before, so it was in the lockdown chat rooms where I really discovered what Direct Provision was, and was really shocked at how terrible it is. One of the most shocking factors is just how long people are kept in limbo.

One common topic that came up was food. Unfortunately a lot of people in centres can't cook for themselves and they were really upset by that. It's a huge part of their identity and heritage. Being denied the right to cook for yourself for several years and being given foods that you might not like, and are often very unhealthy, really eats away at people.

I love cooking and I find it very therapeutic. After a stressful day, I'll get a recipe and cook for an hour and it'll take my mind away from the day's stresses. The chat rooms are where we met Zee, she was always cooking in the background and stuck out to us. I messaged her privately and asked her to lead some cooking classes.

For my day job I was doing lots of online cook-alongs with chefs that work with me. With one chef in particular, I was selling classes, cook-alongs and masterclasses over lockdown. We'd heard of different charities doing similar projects with asylum seekers and refugees to promote integration in London and around the world. So it kind of seemed like a no brainer to give something like that a go here. I didn't see anything that was directly working with people in Direct Provision in that way, and it seems like a good platform to give people a chance to share their culture and heritage.

I pulled Grace in because she's a linguist and there was a group of French people who couldn't understand a lot of the lockdown sessions because they didn't speak English as their first language. Grace speaks French so started attending some of the lockdown info sessions and then was translating it and relaying all the info to the French group.

I presented the idea of BiaFriend in one of the chatrooms and it started from there.

FIADH: I never knew about your French translations, Grace. That's really great. It sounds like a big job.

GRACE: I studied languages and linguistics in University and I have a background in teaching and translation, so I was delighted to help when Caroline mentioned there were some French speaking asylum seekers with some translation needs.

I was working in Vietnam until last year but I moved home before the lockdown. I started attending the lockdown chat rooms and taking notes to relay information and updates back to the group of French speakers.

Unfortunately, many asylum seekers are faced with an enormous language barrier while living in Ireland and it can be very isolating for them, this barrier has been exacerbated since the lockdown. Our hope is that Bia Friend gives asylum seekers a chance to share their culture with people in Ireland, to help them to feel more integrated and also to practice language skills.

Like Caroline, I've always had an interest in food. I had already participated in some online cookalongs during lockdown and I thought the idea of starting some with asylum seekers in Ireland would be really empowering.

I think food is something that we can all easily relate to, no matter where we're from, no matter what our background is, we can all connect with each other through the topic of food.

FIADH: Absolutely. The comfort of food is something we can all relate to. It's universal.

What are your hopes for BiaFriend in the future? The response was massive, wasn't it? I'm assuming you didn't expect it to be so explosive. It was fantastic.

CAROLINE: It's a tricky one to know for sure. We're still piloting the classes. We hope to work with a chef in Cork. She has hopes to expand it into a cookbook at some point, but other than that we're just taking it as it comes at the moment because we both work full time as well. I suppose the pilot was to see if there was an appetite for it, and the answer is definitely yes! We get emails every day asking for more classes, so we must schedule more of them now. We'll definitely continue with it because it's great to see that there's an appetite for it from both sides.

The charity Sanctuary Runners said that, according to a survey they did, 75% of Irish people have never met someone in Direct Provision. It's even more difficult to make that happen now because we're not allowed to go anywhere.

I think BiaFriend is a nice way to make people feel less isolated during this time. It gives people another focus, you know? It's a little boost for mental health as well. It keeps us in touch with everyone as well. Sometimes we might change the class sizes, but it's generally fifteen people from the general public, then five participants from Direct Provision and a cook from Direct Provision.

FIADH: There was a really nice sense of community in the class I sat in on. It felt almost like I was in a kitchen myself, it was so cosy, the only thing missing was the smell.

GRACE: Exactly. We limit the number of participants in each cookalong with the purpose of keeping them interactive and

and sharing that sense of community with each other. We have received such positive feedback from people who have participated in the cookalongs which are not just about learning new recipes but also about sharing stories, learning about new cultures and connecting over our love of food.

We feel really fortunate to be part of Bia Friend and to get to know so many lovely people. Our Bia Friend family is amazing and we can't thank all of the cooks enough for sharing their time and skills with us.

FIADH: Speaking of amazing people, Zee, hello, thank you for coming.

ZEE: I want to tell everybody I'm so happy to be here with beautiful and lovely women. It's such a beautiful day for me and I am so happy. I am in a beautiful period in my life. Since I know these people, I stopped being depressed. I am laughing more, I am doing my hobby and what I like is cooking. So it's beautiful. I am just happy now, you know?
Now I start to think more about my project for the future and start to think about different things that I was never thinking about before because projects like this opened doors for me, or windows, that I can see a little bit out from. Yes, it's a beautiful experience.

FIADH: I'm so glad to see you thriving like this, Zee. In the class that I watched, you made a special type of Algerian couscous dish. Do you have any special memories of preparing it?

zee: Of course, a lot. As an Algerian woman, every Friday we have the tradition to cook couscous in different ways. I have good memories. One of them is after finishing the couscous the kitchen is a mess, big mess. So what happens is, the mothers...like my mother, she takes a big, big plate and she puts all the couscous and all the sauce on the top and we sit down all together and we eat all together. With the buttermilk of course, which is traditional in Algeria. So yeah, it's good memories. I'm still doing it actually. I'm still doing that for my kids and me and I think it's beautiful.

FIADH: It really is. Thank you for sharing that. You said that you stopped your education and started taking over the home kitchen. Can you tell us a little more about that?

zee: Yes, so unfortunately in our country, girls don't have that much choice about their lives. Like we can decide a hundred percent what we need or what we want. It's not just my experience. In my country it's thousands and thousands of girls suffering with the same problem.

When the girl, especially if she's beautiful and her body is nice, unfortunately the parents decide she needs to get married. She needs to make kids and be with a husband and do what the husband says and the mother law.

For me it was like that. I was twelve years old and I was not beautiful, small and white skin, so my father started to say to my mom that I needed to be in the kitchen. Unfortunately at that age, my mother was pregnant with the fifth child, my little sister. She was very sick. The pregnancy; big problem in her bones, she couldn't stand, she couldn't walk. I remember she had a very hard time so I was the only one who helped at home.

I stopped my education. I had no time to go to school, no time to study. I remember coming back from school, I was very small, helping and doing the cleaning and taking care of my brothers. So I decided to stay at home. I felt that my education was useless. I thought, I know the way my life will go.

At fifteen years I was ready and my mom left the kitchen and she gave me all the responsibility of feeding the family. So by the age of fifteen I was cooking, cleaning, doing everything until nineteen.

Then I got married and had my first baby. In Algeria, the woman, if she is married, needs to marry the husband, the mother-in-law, the father-in-law, the brother-in-law, the sister-in-law especially. I had a very difficult life with my marriage.

My situation pushed me to cook. Yeah. This is the way I learned to cook. It's really important in Algeria that the woman cooks different dishes, different sweets, and she needs to satisfy the husband. Especially the husband. He doesn't care at all, if you are tired, sick, or whatever. If the food is not at home, it will be a big problem. And they can even call your father, your mother, and blah, blah, too much problems. Cooking takes a big part in our lives as Algerian women.

This is not the story about all women, just the women who

don't finish studying. Other women survive. Very strong women finish their study and do whatever they want, like working. It's rare you find that. Most of them are just at home cooking and cleaning and make kids. This is our life.

FIADH: That's incredibly strong too, though. Don't forget that. You're a very strong woman. Extremely.

ZEE: Oh, thank you so much. I'm trying my best here. When I came to Ireland I had very difficult years here as an Arabic woman, as Algerian as well. You know, in my country, there is big gate on the window and they are covered with wood. Then big, big curtains, very heavy curtains. So I can't look out. I'm not allowed look out.

So I came here to Ireland, and it was very different. Men can talk to women, you can sit with a man. For me, it was very difficult the first year, especially with my husband. It wasn't that easy. But with time, we're used to the life here and the European style. I'm still fighting. I didn't win yet. But yes, it's not easy as an Arabic woman to live in Europe, but I am trying my best.

But to be honest, since I came here, I feel free. It's you know, that bird was in the cage inside and it gets freedom. So that's what's happened to me. I am free. I am free now. That's why I'm so happy.

FIADH: You're shining. You look incredibly happy.

ZEE: Thank you, so much.

FIADH: You also mentioned during the class that you'd like to work with the homeless in Ireland, can you tell me a bit more about that?

ZEE: When I came here to Ireland, I was living in Balseskin. So I was going sometimes to town, to Dublin. I was seeing people sleeping on the floor. My heart was...I wished to go to the person and hug them and just make them warm. So many times I would go to town and see people like that, sleeping or asking for money, and when I go to the kitchen at Balseskin, I would say to myself, "I am eating warm food and hot food. Did those people have something to eat today?"

I moved here and was talking to people who said they are volunteers with the homeless. So I said, "Yes, in the future I will work as a volunteer." I heard about an Iraqi woman, I'm not sure if it is in Dublin or the UK, but when she got her papers she opened her own office to feed the homeless. I said to myself, "I will be like her," and started to think about the future. I don't know the rules or the laws, so I am thinking, I am imagining and I am dreaming.

FIADH: Thank you for that. I'm so excited for you.

At one point during the class, everyone in their separate kitchens were saying how good the food was smelling. Our sense of smell is meant to have a really strong connection to memories. So, I wanted to finish by asking each of you to share a meal you cook, or one that's been cooked for you, that brings back a special memory.

ZEE: The smell of food? Yeah, of course. I miss my mother. The smell of food brings a lot of memories; my mother cooking, my grandmother cooking. So every time I cook anything, especially when my kids come to me and say, "Mommy, the food is delicious!" the memories come. We love my mother's food, she's very good at cooking. I get it all from her.

GRACE: That's so beautiful Zineb. I think for me, it's something similar. The smell of freshly baked scones and brown bread brings back fond memories from my childhood. We grew up in a household with a lot of baking so these smells trigger happy memories for me. What do you think, Caroline?

CAROLINE: Yes, I think the same. Our mum was a chef before she had kids and she always made fresh Brown bread and stuff. I've tried to do it since, but I haven't mastered it as well as she used to make it.

ZEE: Brown bread? Since I came to Ireland I started to make brown bread. I just fell in love. I never had it in my country. When I came I started making brown bread, scones, even apple crumble. It's just absolutely beautiful. I love Irish food.

I don't want my girls to go through what I did when I was small. I want them to have education and freedom.

Zee

Zee is the mother of five beautiful children did Level 5 Childcare and Education. Her dream is to cook and provide food for the homeless. Zee has been living in Direct Provision for over six years.

Caroline McCarthy

Caroline lived in London for 5 years working in food marketing. She worked voluntarily with charities that help asylum seekers and refugees including Breadwinners, The Refugee Council and Homes for Syrians. She launched BiaFriend with her sister Grace in early 2021. The project consists of cooking lessons taught by asylum seekers and refugees to promote integration in Ireland.

"Cooking is also great for our mental health, something everyone can benefit from during these unprecedented times. We are delighted to be able to use our free time and skills to create more awareness and connect with people through our love of food."

Grace McCarthy

Last year, Grace returned to Ireland after working in Vietnam. She studied Languages and Translation at University so assists French speakers in Direct Provision with translation needs. "Language can be an enormous barrier for asylum seekers living in Ireland so I am happy to help where possible."

With both sisters returned to Ireland, she and Caroline were delighted to run Bia Friend in their spare time as a platform for outreach and integration. Bia Friend also gives our friends in Direct Provision a chance to improve their language skills and to grow in confidence. We can see many beautiful friendships and connections blossoming from Bia Friend and are hopeful for the future.

See more from BiaFriend:
 WEBSITE - biafriend.com
 INSTAGRAM - @biafriend

ALL HOPE IS NOT LOST
Moving forward from current media trends.

Mairead Sheehy

Direct Provision is a buzzword that has cropped up many times in Irish media over the past decade. It has been covered vastly by the media and been the centre of many a headline, article, and radio package. However, media coverage of Direct Provision has not always been as extensive as many would have liked, often leaving out crucial information and statements made by those affected most. It is believed that the media often does not accurately portray the true extent of the hardship endured by residents in these centres.

It is striking how few articles in the media have featured interviews conducted with asylum seekers living in these conditions in order to get a first-hand response, allowing them to utilise the platform to voice their experience. This is evident in how the mental health and wellbeing of those residents is portrayed. The media touches on the negative implications associated with being cooped up in such a soul-shattering environment, but only scrapes the surface when it comes to the true extent of what is occurring behind closed doors.

An article published by journal.ie on the 26th of May 2019, outlines the dire need for vulnerability assessments, which are required by law to be completed on each individual upon entering the country. These are necessary for monitoring and determining the mental capacity of individuals on a one to one basis.

Nick Henderson of the Irish Refugee Council has said, "Each person, under law, should have had this [vulnerability] assessment within 30 days of making their asylum application, to identify if they are vulnerable and what additional supports they need. [...] This has not happened."

The media touches on the topic of poor mental health occurring in residents as a result of living in these inhumane conditions. However, this is only the tip of the iceberg. The mental health of asylum seekers is at an all time low.

According to a recent article published in The Irish Times, Ireland has one of the highest rates of mental health illness in Europe, ranking joint third out of the thirty-six countries surveyed. The rate of depression in Ireland is also well above the European average for both Irish men and women. Another shocking fact revealed in the article was that in 2016, approximately 18.5% of the Irish population were recorded as having a mental health disorder such as bipolar, anxiety, depression, schizophrenia or drug or alcohol use.

Think about it this way; many of us struggle with poor mental health from time to time in our everyday lives and go through periods of feeling low and uneasy. If we were placed in prison-like conditions where our freedom was taken away and living in boredom day-in day out, the negative implications on our mental health would be indescribable. This is what is occurring daily for residents. It does not take a genius to work this out. Our country has well and truly failed them.

Words cannot describe how disappointed I am in this failed system. It is truly upsetting to read about these individuals who fled such dangerous countries, in hope of a better life and a fresh start, yet they are greeted with these inhumane conditions. For many asylum seekers, Ireland was dreamt of as the light at the end of the tunnel, the peace amidst the threatening storm. Unfortunately, the reality is the complete opposite, filled with tension and sadness; leaving many wondering why they ever risked their lives to come here.

Another heavily criticised aspect of Direct Provision centres, yet hardly ever covered by the media, is the quality of the food served to residents. The true extent of this is rarely touched on by mainstream outlets.

Asylum seekers have revealed the barbaric rules they must follow when it comes to cooking, a lack of nutritious food, and rigid mealtimes, proving especially difficult for families with young children living in the centres. There is very little information available detailing meals such as these, leading me to assume that the majority of people on the outside are unaware life in these centres is as dictatorial and brutal as it is.

It is hard to imagine not being allowed to prepare one's own food, and many are completely reliant on the insufficient meals provided by the centre. This is completely degrading and most definitely in breach of the resident's human rights.

Article 1 of The Universal Declaration of Human Rights states that, "All human beings are born free and equal in dignity and rights. They are endowed with reason and conscience and should act towards one another in a spirit of brotherhood." The lack of dignity experienced by residents in these centres is appalling. So much so, that the words dignity and Direct Provision centre do not belong together in the same sentence. Sharing a cramped living space with a complete stranger with inadequate privacy to undress and freshen up is not a dignified experience. In fact, it is the complete opposite. It is information like this that needs to be on the front covers of national papers and broadcast by the media, informing everyone of this country's wrongdoings. The media's silence is deafening.

Aramark Corporation is a company privately contracted to run three state-owned Direct Provision centres accommodating up to 900 asylum seekers. These three centres include Kinsale Road, Co. Cork, Knockalisheen, Co. Clare and Athlone in Co. Westmeath. Aramark is the largest prison catering company in the USA, having contracts with 500 correctional facilities. How fitting it is that, just across the water, Aramark is in control of Direct Provision centres with living conditions that can closely resemble that of a prison.

Aramark owns over 50% of market shares of the food services industry in Ireland. This consists of supplies to universities, hospitals, Croke Park and Direct Provision centres. Since the year 2000, Aramark has received €155 million from the running of these centres.

Despite being a billion dollar global empire, Aramark provides sub-standard food, allowing them to directly profit off creating deplorable living standards for human beings. This is not something to be proud of. Aramark are shamelessly profiting off of the vulnerable members in society across the globe; with reports of maggots found in prison food in the US.

This company, although merely hired by the government to provide a service, proves to be immoral and lacks compassion in its delivery and harmful practices. Money or tight budgets are not an issue for this multi-billion dollar corporation with Aramark's global revenue in 2019 summing up to a grand $16.2 billion total. The company has the funds to afford to provide much higher-quality meals and services to asylum seekers but chooses not to.

The media has failed time and time again to criticize this money-hungry company that is responsible for much of the hardship endured by the residents. It's impossible to fathom that today such inequality exists right under our noses, in every county of the country. We as a nation should not stand for this.

According to an article by *The Irish Times* published on the 9th of November 2018, the students at the University of Limerick were a step ahead of the game, when they made the bold decision to boycott all Aramark-affiliated businesses on campus. In a piece published in the UL newspaper, *An Focal*, Siofra Guerin accuses the contractors of Direct Provision centres of providing "poor services to keep costs down and generate more profit," citing Aramark catering as one of these businesses. She writes that the food group has a strong presence on campus with concessions including Starbucks, Subway, Chopped, Costa, Eden and Mexican Kitchen.

Although it can be disheartening to notice the media seemingly sit back and say nothing about these businesses, all hope is not lost. If you are angered by these facts do not let the moment pass, make a conscious decision to boycott Aramark owned businesses. These include all retail and cafe outlets of the Irish company Avoca, which was purchased by Aramark in 2015, Capital Dock in Dublin 4, Cork's English Market, the Ilac Centre, Blackrock Shopping Centre, Beacon

South Quarter in Sandyford, the Irish Life Centre and much more. I urge everyone to do their research and educate yourselves on these businesses, trying to avoid them where at all possible.

If you are wondering what you can do to help individuals living in these awful conditions, look no further. There are many initiatives that have been set up in order to directly help those living in Direct Provision centres. *DP Donations* is an Instagram page created by two UCC students in order to collect necessary items to be donated directly to residents living in these centres. These girls have done tremendous work organising drop-offs and collections across the country and working side by side with the residents in order to try and fulfill any special requests they have as best they can. *DP Drops Ireland* is another page which has organised drop-offs of invaluable goods to centres all over the country; from Dublin to Kerry. They have provided sanitary items to women that were in need and collect school items for young children. Having all of these things is second-nature to us but when faced with a tiny budget and overpriced items on sale in the centre, many of these items are difficult to source.

The Hygiene Bank is another campaign set up by a group of volunteers in order to collect and donate hygiene products all over Ireland. These pages have had huge success rates and gathered a good following of interested people along the way, all eager to help out.

If you take away anything from this, give these pages a follow and take a look at the phenomenal work they have accomplished. You never know, you might discover they have a collection point near you and feel inspired to donate some items or perhaps a bag of clothes after a wardrobe clear out. Many of these accounts also have GoFundMe or Patreon links in their bios. You can also help by informing others of this information. Discuss Aramark with friends and family and highlight the horrendous conditions asylum seekers endure and give them the tools to research more about this and inform themselves. Have the conversation. Don't allow others to be blissfully unaware. The time is now.

The Irish media has, in the past, failed the general public by not informing us of the true extent of human rights abuses in Direct Provision centres. We have been kept out of the loop. The media has failed asylum seekers miserably in lacking to report on and inform the public of the difficult conditions and routines endured by so many individuals day in day out. It is the media's silence that has prevented people from realising how atrocious these conditions truly are. We rely on the media to be informed of what is happening in the world yet somehow we have been kept in the dark.

We cannot let this progress any further. Another day endured by asylum seekers in these harrowing centres is a day too many. It is not enough to sit back and complain. We must take the situation into our own hands and fight for change. We are the future.

Mairead Sheehy

Mairead Sheehy studied Journalism and New Media at the University of Limerick. She completed her placement with *The Kerryman* newspaper and enjoys using her writing to raise awareness for a variety of social issues. Mairead has never shied away from writing about what she believes in, often finding a thrill in speaking openly about more 'taboo' issues.

We all the residents of Skellig Star Hotel are embarking on Hunger Strike until we are moved out of here to appropriate Accommodation
28th July 2020

It is almost four consecutive months of living in an inhumane condition at Skellig Star Hotel Direct provision and the past and present government has not done anything to help us from this open prison.

We have sent emails several times highlighting how we have suffered physically, socially, mentally and emotionally due to the treatment received in the hands of IPAS during covid and post covid.

We have been traumatized and for us to recover from this we need to be all moved out of this accommodation immediately by the Ministers(Deputy Gorman and Deputy McEntee) to appropriate accommodation centres. We are just 41 ASYLUM SEEKERS remaining including 7 children. More than 30 asylum seekers left the centre to different parts of the country because they preferred to be on the street than to continue live here.

Our demands are as follows;

1. Access to Social worker in order to have our health catered for and monitored regularly.

2. Transfer of all the residents to appropiate accommodation centre where we can have proper vulnerability assessment and get adequate treatment for trauma.

3. Preferred place of accommodation centre with adequate facilities are:

MOSNEY ACCOMMODATION CENTRE

TULLAMORE ACCOMMODATION CENTRE.

"Suffering by nature or chance never seems so painful as suffering inflicted on us by the arbitrary will of another"

Waiting is painful,forgetting is the most painful.

....

Residents of
Skellig Star Hotel Direct Provision Center,
Cahersiveen
Email: SkelligstarhotelCahersiveen@protonmail.com

SKELLIG STAR ACCOMMODATION CENTRE
How the rushed opening of a Kerry Direct Provision Centre failed the local community and the asylum seekers it was meant to protect

Eamonn Hickson

In March 2020, as the coronavirus crisis initially gripped the country, the Department of Justice transported 105 asylum seekers to the former Skellig Star Hotel in a small town in South-West Kerry. The local community and public representatives voiced their concerns; moving these people to a hotel in Cahersiveen was in direct contradiction to the advice public health officials were giving. The public were being told to socially distance, avoid large social gatherings, and be mindful that creating and maintaining space between people was a cheap and effective antidote to the coronavirus. Yet, 105 asylum seekers were put on buses from Dublin to Cahersiveen, where the Department of Justice was adamant that the residents would be safe.

A month later, there were four confirmed cases of Covid-19 in the former hotel. The following week, there were twenty cases. By the end of June, Cahersiveen had the second-highest number of confirmed Covid-19 cases in Kerry.

Disconnect is a word that was used a lot during this tumultuous period. It was claimed that there was a disconnect between the residents of the Skellig Star Accommodation Centre and government departments. I don't feel that this was the correct word. Disconnect implies that there was a link established at some point, but it had since been severed. As a local journalist, I was familiar with this story from the outset and it could never be claimed a strong connection existed between government departments and the Cahersiveen community or residents at any point.

I prefer to use ignorance; a lack of knowledge or information. The Department of Justice had a number of asylum seekers and a set amount of space. I don't believe anyone in the department acted maliciously when deciding to send 105 people to a former hotel in South Kerry to stay in rooms with non-family members during a historic pandemic, rooms which adhered to dimensions set out in an Act from the 1960s.

Were the residents, locals and media outlets too critical of the Department of Justice? Did department officials just do what had to be done? Maybe so. The residents of the Skellig Star were not the only people the department had a duty of care for, and the centre wasn't the only one in Ireland. Indeed, it was one of seven centres in Kerry at the time.

Cahersiveen and the Iveragh Peninsula have suffered badly in recent decades due to rural depopulation. The small town, which has a population of just over 1,000 people, is on the Ring of Kerry tourist route, but doesn't get the volume of overnight stays that more well-known stops like Killarney or Kenmare receive.

The stark effects of a dwindling population are everywhere. From having to amalgamate with neighbours in the underage Gaelic football competitions due to poor numbers, to seeing dozens of vacant buildings around the area. The secondary school, Coláiste Na Sceilge, was designed towards the end of the last century. It catered for students from Derrynane to Dromid, Glenbeigh to Portmagee, and was built to accommodate a large student population. Now, it's akin to a child slipping on their father's size elevens.

At first, it was the graduates who left for third level or work elsewhere, but they always returned. In recent years, their children followed the well-worn tracks outward but never came back. They couldn't. People need opportunities to work, to integrate into the community, to live. Cahersiveen, like many rural areas of Ireland, is suffering an ongoing exodus, one which has left many towns and villages stripped of vibrancy, stripped of opportunity, stripped of life.

It was this environment that the department put 105 residents into, an environment that gave no glimmer of a happy ending. Locals welcomed the residents. However, they had a major issue. What was the reality of the residents' future, once the pandemic was overcome? Where would they work? How would they travel around the community with such poor public transport? What aspect of living in a new (and rural) community could they find purpose in? Make no mistake, the people of Cahersiveen supported the residents throughout the ordeal, but they had concerns of the long-term viability of the ill-conceived plan. They told me that a smaller number would have made more sense.

Running concurrently to the residents' worries was the issue of the hotel's previous ownership. Kerry TD Michael Healy-Rae was among the most vocal in his opposition to the centre. It transpired that he had sold his share of the hotel's lease in December 2019 to the centre's new operator. One of the two other shareholders was a man named Jude Kirk. Deputy Healy-Rae denied knowing what the new operator intended to do with the hotel once ownership was transferred.

The residents' struggles became more pressing in mid-April, when the first cases were announced. A few days later, while I was at work, I received a call from Independent deputy Michael Healy-Rae. He had confirmation from the HSE that further cases had been diagnosed in the centre.

Around this time, I sent a Freedom of Information Act request to the Department of Justice. In the newsroom, we simply call these FOIs. They're one of the few tools we have in forcing government departments and public bodies to give information that the public has a right to know. My request was relatively simple: all correspondence received or sent by the department during the period January 1st 2019 to mid-April 2020.

Most of what it revealed was known already. *The Kerryman* newspaper had heard a rumour that there were plans to move residents to Cahersiveen in January, something the Department denied at the time. However, the information I received showed that there were plans even earlier to move residents to the former hotel.

In September 2019, a department official had inspected the hotel for its suitability as a Direct Provision centre. It was open as a hotel at the time. In October 2019, there were plans to open it as a Direct Provision centre in November, with a capacity for 300 residents. There are over fifty rooms in the hotel and thirty-six apartments out the back. The opening was delayed until January 2020 and then went quiet until March 9th when the department reignited the proposal again. Four days later, the contract was ready to be signed between the new operator and the department. Within a week, buses were leaving Dublin, destined for Cahersiveen.

My radio colleagues Jerry O'Sullivan and Treasa Murphy on the Kerry Today show kept the public informed of the latest happenings, along with Mick Clifford writing for the Irish Examiner and Sinead Kelleher for The Kerryman, amongst others. But, a sense of helplessness did exist. How much notice were Department officials and the Minister for Justice Charlie Flanagan taking of all this? I'm pretty sure they didn't have the Radio Kerry app on their phones and it's easy to mute certain people on Twitter.

The residents and locals were staging protests, which we and other media reported. But how much did it matter to those who were making the decisions? How easy was it for the department officials to scroll away from it on their feeds? Minister Flanagan had to do something.

In May 2020, Flanagan published an open letter in the local papers and spoke with Jerry that morning on Kerry Today. When being questioned on how this was all allowed to happen, the minister said, "I'm not going to get into the blame game." To which Jerry replied, "Why not?"

We weren't seeking scapegoats, we weren't seeking people's heads, we were seeking answers. Asylum seekers, many of whom had fled war-torn and unstable countries, were being let down by a system created to help them. While it may have been unintended, it didn't happen by accident. It's not easy to hold your hand up after making a mistake and admitting you were wrong. The Department should have done this in mid-April, following the outbreak. Instead, it took another month for the minister to address it publicly and a further two months before the new minister took action.

Further FOIs showed that some healthcare professionals were concerned about the situation. A specialist in public health medicine told the Department of Justice that it was unacceptable to keep the Direct Provision residents in their rooms 24 hours per day.

On the 28th April 2020, Dr Anne Sheahan, Consultant in Public Health, noted a number of concerns. She said the residents had no privacy from the public due to the centre's streetside position; the only lift in the building was small and unmonitored; and there was only a small yard out back which the residents were unable to use because of building materials. She also said this would mean keeping them in their rooms 24 hours a day, as there was no other area to allow residents to take brief exercise. Dr Sheahan concluded that these conditions were unacceptable.

On May 7th, the person tasked with using contactless thermometers in the centre emailed Louise Carlton, Clinical Nurse Specialist in Infectious Diseases, saying that the two thermometers given by the HSE were not working. Mick Clifford, writing for The Examiner, said temporary heaters had to be brought from Tralee in March as the heating system in the hotel didn't function properly. These occurrences added to the residents' worries.

Behind the scenes, there were various storylines developing. The Department of Justice refused an offer of free self-catering accommodation for residents in the centre, saying the offeror had no experience in caring for those seeking asylum. On May 13th, a previous co-holder of the lease wrote to the Department, offering eight homes

25km from the Skellig Star Accommodation Centre in Cahersiveen while a "better option [was] being sought for asylum seekers and their children." The Department refused, saying it knew Mr Kirk was a 50% beneficiary of the deal that saw the hotel change hands and it didn't want to get involved in any issues between other parties. It also said Mr Kirk had no first-hand knowledge or experience in the care of international protection applicants. It added that Mr Kirk was, in effect, asking the Department to close down the business Mr Kirk had sold to someone and transfer it to him – albeit free of charge – without addressing who would feed residents, transport them, what standard of care would be available and how sustainable it would be.

Meanwhile, local and national politicians and interest groups were raising the plight of the centre's residents on a near-daily basis. Sinn Féin TD Pa Daly described the minimum standards for room dimensions, which the department still adheres to, as being a little larger than a double bed. Fianna Fáil TD and later elected Minister for Education Norma Foley said she had evidence Covid-19 was transported to the centre by bus. Councillors Norma Moriarty and Michael Cahill were among the local representatives voicing their concerns.

In June, I travelled to South Kerry for a Sunday drive. I made a little detour when driving through Cahersiveen. It started raining as I drove past the Skellig Star, onto the nearby Legal Aid Board offices, the museum that would look more suited to a Disney film, across the bridge and up towards a soccer pitch across the water. Then the rain turned torrential. As I returned over the bridge, two residents of the Skellig Star were being soaked, caught in the burst of rain. I stopped, lowered the window and asked if they needed a drive. They politely refused, saying they were okay in the rain.

It got me thinking, as I passed the centre again; was there some freedom in the downpour, a freedom that didn't exist within the building. A building with small rooms, the single elevator, the exercise yard out back half-covered in building materials, the faulty heating system and the recent memory of positive cases.

At the end of July, most of the residents went on hunger strike. It was the beginning of the end of the Skellig Star Accommodation Centre. It's difficult to tell what would have happened were it not for their courage…and desperation.

The Skellig Star Accommodation Centre and the heartache it represented was made real when I found out residents' names, when I heard their voices on our station, when I met two of them in the downpour – and maybe that was the reason for the differing levels of empathy. How connected can you be to someone when you're in Dublin, they're in Cahersiveen and the only contact you have is through leaflets you've had printed and taped to their doors?

The new Minister for Justice, Helen McEntee, made a promise at the end of July that the residents would be moved from the centre by the year's end. In September, 168 days after the residents first entered the Skellig Star Accommodation Centre in Cahersiveen, the last of them left Heartbreak Hotel.

Eamonn Hickson

Eamonn is a news and sports journalist with *Radio Kerry*. Prior to the 2008 downturn, he qualified as a civil engineer and had begun a career in construction. Following the financial crisis, Eamonn went back to college and attained a degree in creative writing. Eamonn has published three novels in recent years. He was awarded the Law Society's Justice Media Newcomer of the Year award in 2019, the GAA's MacNamee radio award in 2020. Eamonn also holds seven Guinness World Records in the health and fitness field.

See more of Eamonn's Work:

Website - www.radiokerry.ie

Instagram - @the_hiksons

Article written for @letshelpdirectprovision 02/02/2021

Mosney Hunger Strike

An asylum seeker* abstained from eating and drinking in a week-long hunger strike against the State's policies on asylum seekers' right to work.

Sarah Hamilton
*Name has been changed to
'A' for identity protection

"My son, I have a feeling that it's the last time I will see you. I will never see you again". These were the last words spoken by A's father before A fled their home and made their way to Ireland. Today marks the sixth day that the asylum seeker has been on hunger strike. Based in a Direct Provision centre in Mosney, Co. Meath, A has declared that they are willing to go on hunger strike until death, if the Government does not grant them the right to work in Ireland so that they can provide for their family.

A left their elderly parents at home. Their father has health conditions, including Alzheimer's disease. Their mother has been unable to pay their rent for months and was seen by a neighbour rooting through trash cans in an attempt to source food, which A was informed of via WhatsApp. Announcing the Strike, A said that they were willing to die, "Because I die a thousand times every day while I am watching my parents die of oppression, hunger and illnesses." Speaking with *LMFM News*, A said, "If I cannot support my family, they will die. I prefer to die before them."

The solicitor fled their homeland after suffering devastating consequences when they appeared on a political television show. After criticizing the constitution, A was arrested by the ruling regime where they were detained and then tortured for months. A's spouse-to-be was also tortured and unfortunately did not survive the brutal mistreatment. A was finally released on the conditions that they would join the army to fight in the Civil War. Since A refused, the threat on their life was so strong that they escaped to Ireland in the hopes of a better future.

A arrived in Ireland in August 2020. Current regulations set by the Department of Justice state that an asylum seeker cannot work until they have been in Ireland for six months. A was given a temporary residency card when they arrived. When they attempted to apply for a work permit, A was told by immigration authorities that the residency card had expired.

Hence, the government has denied their application for a work permit. A has appealed this decision, but there have been many cases where asylum seekers are left waiting years for their residency card to be renewed. In fact, some of the asylum seekers who share residency in the Mosney centre with A have been waiting as long as six years. This pigeon-holes asylum seekers into a poverty trap, where they are unable to provide for themselves or their families.

A more than fits the description of an asylum seeker that is vulnerable and at risk of self-harm. Complications with their right to work may only push them into this category further. A has spoken of the many mental health issues they have been left with as a result of their trauma, including PTSD, insomnia and depression. The Beacon cited such delays by the government as "legalized cruelty."

<u>WHAT HAPPENS TO THE BODY ON HUNGER STRIKE?</u>

Hunger strikes have been used as desperate pleas by asylum seekers to be heard by government bodies for many years. But what are the physical effects of such protest?

The Lancet, a British medical journal states that if a person is also refusing liquids, including water, "deterioration is very rapid, with death quite possible within seven to fourteen days. Low levels of thiamine (vitamin B1) become a real risk after two or three weeks and can result in severe neurological problems, including cognitive impairment, vision loss and lack of motor skills." It also cites the psychological effects of hunger strike, including impulsivity. The Journal of Medical Ethics states that these effects can "enhance the likelihood that strikers will starve themselves to death."

There are reports that emergency services were called to the centre on Monday evening after A had not eaten for five days. In a statement issued on Monday evening, the Department of Justice said that it cannot comment on any individual immigration or international protection cases for confidentiality reasons.

Originally, asylum seekers had to wait nine months before they could apply for work. But on the 28th of January 2021, The Minister for Justice, Helen McEntee TD, announced new measures that allow applicants to seek work six months after they make their application.

The TD also extended the applicant's permission to work from six months to twelve months. However, the extensively long waiting time seen in many cases for asylum seekers to have their residency cards renewed makes their ability to work a complex and somewhat impossible goal to reach. Also, there is little known for the future of those in Direct Provision after their yearly allowance of work has ended.

A spokesperson for The Department of Justice declared that, "Anyone who has a query about their application for international protection should contact the International Protection Office directly for an update in confidence."

This is not the first time residents in Direct Provision have gone on hunger strike. A DP centre in Sligo had residents go on hunger strike for thirty five days. A has already surpassed the Kerry hunger strikers of March last year, who went three days without any food.

Sarah Hamilton

Sarah holds a First-Class Honours in Creative Writing with University College Dublin. She has had pieces published in Pilcrow and Dagger, The Oval, The Galway Review, and as a returning writer and Society editor for Cassandra Voices magazine. Today, she is writing a novel and works as a writer for *Let's Help*, an organisation that provides supplies to those in Direct Provision centres. In her spare time, she volunteers as a phone counsellor for Dublin Rape Crisis Centre. Sarah hopes to engage young audiences with injustices in Irish society. She is keen on using the written word to educate people on Direct Provision.

Sarah Recommends:

Books

This Hostel Life by Melatu Uche Okorie

Elizabeth's Story - My Childhood was Ripped Away - The Irish Times

Let's Help Blog: *Mental Health and Direct Provision*

See more of Sarah's Work:

Website - www.letshelpdirectprovision.com/blog

Instagram - @wildegal / @letshelpdirectprovision

INSTITUTIONALISED LIVING IN IRELAND
Investigating the parallels between the horrific institutional living conditions experienced in Magdalene Laundries and Mother and Baby Homes, with today's Direct Provision system.

Mary-Kate Slattery

It is no secret that Ireland has a shameful past when it comes to institutionalism, clerical abuse and the insidious shaming and abuse of our women. It is something that should never have happened. The trauma experienced by these survivors is more than anyone should ever have to deal with in a lifetime. That trauma is now ours to deal with.

To this day, the government is failing these women through a lack of transparency and false promises. It produces reports and commissions that never serve to heal, but only to partially record and meddle with the past. They are failing these women through state apologies that fail to place the blame on the individuals and institutions that are genuinely culpable. There have been too many of these half-hearted attempts to heal our hideous history and it is exacerbated by the overwhelming lack of honesty and transparency.

It is paramount to understand our social and political failure, as the Irish Nation and how much we as a society have evolved in our understanding and implementation of egalitarian societal norms. It is equally important to revisit and reflect upon our recent, and in many ways forgotten, past. Ireland has carried a hideous and insidious past when it comes to the history of institutionalised living. Our historical consciousness and engagement with the criminological element of institutions like the Magdalene Laundries is profoundly under-developed. There is still to this day a striking absence in full engagement with the painful history of these institutions within our public discourse.

The Threat of Female Sexuality and Power

Female sexuality has long been fundamental to women's experiences of social control. As it has well been documented, women in Ireland in the 20th Century who were regarded as having engaged in, or suspected to be engaging in, sexual behaviour deemed 'inappropriate' found themselves commonly confined to convents, homes or penitentiaries.

In their writing on 'Coercive Confinement' in Ireland, O'Donnell and O'Sullivan both studied the experiences of unmarried mothers and the so-called 'fallen women' of Ireland. In their examination, they submit data that shows that the number of women confined to normal prisons was minuscule in comparison to the number of women confined to asylums like the Magdalene Laundries. For example, in the year 1951, data records that 2,003 women were confined in Magdalene Laundries or mother and baby homes, whereas only forty-three women were confined to prison. Christina Quinlan describes, the Magdalene Laundry asylums as "the carceral appendage of the convent [...] used for over a century to encourage conformity in non-conforming women."

The existence of these State-sanctioned institutions propagated and enforced a Catholic construction of sexuality in a gendered project which dedicated almost all actions to controlling women. This disciplining superstructure was designed to produce 'decent' women, by limiting women's access to work and public spaces, and reducing their existence to the marital home. When this view was transcended, it was met with threats of new sites of reformation and emigration if they failed to conform.

Female Sexuality, it seems, was linked, in the public mind, with deviance. It is written in the 1937 constitution, that women by their 'life,' not as their 'work,' in the home support the state to the point of which without it the common good cannot be achieved.

Linda Connolly refers to this fact as "[a] cool and dispassionate historical interpretation of this clause suggests that it simply reflects the social order of the day. Women were in reality confined to the sphere of the home and family; feminists of the time were 'exceptional' and marginal women who did not reflect the overall experience of Irish women."

It was submitted by Dr. Maryann Valiulis that the period of the formation of the Irish Free State between 1920s and the 1930s, was a powerful time for the construction of strong gender roles. She argues these roles were born from a discrepancy between the gender roles during the period of revolution and the traditional and rigid roles that were met with the settling of the post-revolutionary period. She argues that after Ireland gained independence, it birthed traditional gender roles of male as paterfamilias and women as the domesticated homemaker.

History of the Magdalene Laundries

The Magdalene Laundries first emerged in the mid 18th Century. They were institutions run by nuns of the Catholic Church. These institutions had the initial aim in the 1700s to be a sanctuary. The first Magdalene Asylum opened in 1767 on Leeson Street in Dublin. When Ireland was first colonized by England, we experienced large shifts and changes as a society.

We experienced economic and territorial re-organisation; our geography changed. We experienced new divisions in the workforce, and in the re-organisation of capitalist structures like farming. We also experienced a redefinition of social norms, all of which lend itself to the development, post-independence, of an oppressive Catholic Ireland. With this developed a Catholic counter- culture in which women had less of a voice in society. Women were treated as second class citizens, and the Catholic Church ruled virtually unchallenged.

With the establishment of the Irish Free State and the devastating effect of the civil war, there was a conscious attempt made by the government to differentiate the nation with what was considered 'British'. Ireland was promoted as a Catholic and morally pure country, and anyone who transcended the new ideals set out for the Free State was to be apprehended and hidden. An example of one such character was the unmarried mother.

The Catholic-Counter Culture Shift in Post-Independent Ireland

We are brought up through the school system learning about Irish freedom, however it was not all positive. Irish society observed a surge in conservatism as a result of Catholic counter-culture in 1922.

When Ireland gained independence, Catholicism became an intrinsic part of our national identity. Catholicism was what differentiated us from our colonisers. Catholicism quickly saturated our laws and sociological norms at the formation of the Irish Free State in 1922. As Maraid Enwright states, "in the post-colonial state, Catholicism became the defining characteristic of Irishness, understood in opposition to Englishness."

In post-independent Ireland, the Magdalene Laundries intended to maintain social and moral order, and at the time were widely believed to be achieving that goal. The name of the asylums, 'Magdalene Laundries,' originated from the biblical Mary Magdalene, as James M. Smith stated in 2008. Smith observes Mary Magdalene as the prime example of atonement and spiritual renewal, which aligns with the expectations upon the women confined in the Laundries. The biblical woman is said to have once been corrupted by evil spirits and cleansed by the power of purity possessed by Jesus Christ. She was reformed in holiness.

The McAleese Report and Omissions

Between the years of 1922 and 1996, it has been estimated by the researchers of The McAleese Report that more than 14,000 oppressed women, some as young as nine, were confined to the Laundries to carry out unpaid forced labour as well as being subjected to psychological and physical abuse by the nuns who ran the institutions. "Many women were institutionalised and incarcerated for decades on end, living lives of total isolation from their communities and society at large."

They were run as profitable commercial businesses in a post-independent Ireland, which meant they were significantly influenced by the rise of the capitalist world system and transformed between 1767-1996 as forced labour asylums.

James M. Smith submits that these super-structure institutions were not solely Catholic, but reflective of the place of women in society beyond a Catholic viewpoint. An example that reflects the discrimination toward women in Ireland at this time can be observed in the words of the Minister for Industry and Commerce in the Seanad in 1955: "the persons concerned here are not ordinary factory workers. They are miscreants of one kind or another. They are people who are in there, in these institutions, for the public good." This explicitly depicts the the official attitude towards Magdalene girls and women at that time.

Another way to highlight the sociological view of these institutions is through reading the parliamentary debates on the Criminal Justice Act in 1960. This Act allowed the courts to use these institutions outside of the formal criminal justice system.

The Magdalene Laundries officially became sites to which the courts could send young female offenders instead of to prisons. O'Donnell and O'Sullivan submit that the origins of this legislative provision lies in a meeting which was held in 1957. This meeting involved Taoiseach Eamon De Valera and the Archbishop of Dublin John Charles McQuaid, showing the grasp that the Catholic Church held over the new State. As Dr. Maeve O'Rourke has stated, "This is not a question of applying today's standards to the past; it was illegal at the time."

Even at the time, it would not have been lawful for Laundries to have gained profits from exploiting these unpaid workers.

THE UNITED NATIONS COMMITTEE AGAINST TORTURE

It was submitted in the Concluding Observations of the United Nations Committee Against Torture, that the Irish State failed to afford protections to these women and honour their fundamental human rights and individual liberty.

They noted that it should be expected that, in a democratic society, the State would fulfill their duties to these women. To prevent them being held against their will, not to exploit their forced labour, and to protect these women's rights to a safe workplace, to social welfare and an education. This grave maltreatment of women continued right up until the final Laundry closed on October 25th 1996.

The McAleese Report was criticised for a number of reasons after it was published in 2013. As James Gallon stated in Law and Gender in Modern Ireland, "[t]he conducts of the findings of the McAleese Committee risk exacerbating the discriminatory and gendered forms of harm experienced by the victim-survivors of the Laundries."

Prior to the investigation, the victim-survivors were told that the redress board would investigate in a non-adversarial way. However, it was stated by Clare McGettrick of Justice for Magdalenes that the manner in which the committee interviewed survivors of the Laundries was adversarial and traumatic.

CONCLUSION

Silence is something that comes so naturally to Irish people, silence that is born from shame. It is clear to see how, without active engagement and constant calls for civil engagement, that it is very easy for it to go unchallenged. We also need to engage with reminders of our painful past in Ireland when it comes to institutional living in order to tackle the present.

We have enormous amounts of work to do to this day to honor the horrific treatment of the survivors of these former institutions. Just as we have to tear apart the Direct Provision system at any chance we can until change for the better is made. One of the major learnings we can take from observing the past and applying to the present, is highlighting the need for transparency above all else when it comes to reports and commissions that serve to heal.

Transparency when it comes to apologies from Heads of State. Transparency when it comes to government objectives and timelines to abolish such a hideous system that is denied so many people of their rights to live a full and meaningful life. Amongst other things, it is the commitment to transparency that is paramount to see positive change in this country.

Mary-Kate Slattery

Mary-Kate is a masters student in Trinity College Dublin in the area of Peace Studies and Conflict Resolution. Her background is in Law, and in 2020, specialised her research in feminist criminology. Her dissertation focused on 'The Forced Labour in Magdalene Laundries' where she also examined the omissions of the McAleese report. She now works in Seanad E´ireann as a legislative and policy researcher with Senator Frances Black. Mary-Kate is also a champion Irish boxer and mental health advocate.

See more of Mary-Kate's Work:
    INSTAGRAM - @mkslattery

QUESTIONING THE POWER AND AUTHORITY OF RACIAL BOUNDARIES
Why identity matters.

Gabrielle Fullam

Race and ethnicity are not immutable fixed characteristics. Rather, they are a complex combination of political and social circumstances. Against a political backdrop which allows both states and individuals to discriminate against people on the basis of their race, ethnicity, or citizenship background – we must question what these labels actually mean. A brief evaluation of mixed-race terminology will be provided as an example for politicisation of identity.

WHY IDENTITY MATTERS: PRIVILEGE AND PENALTY

When commenting on the 2014 Black Lives Matter protests in Ferguson, Zizek (2016) proposes that it has become evident the "police effectively function as a force of occupation" in Black communities. Zizek goes on to comment that the domestic police behave "like that of a force trying to control a foreign population." These protests, their cause, and the state's reaction to them, are generally seen as totemic symbols of racialisation and racial mistreatment at the hands of the state, but these comments signal something deeper about our common conception of race.

The problem, to an outsider, is not just the rampant mistreatment of people of colour at the hands of the arms of the US government, but that this mistreatment itself can be likened to the state's treatment towards non-nationals (foreigners, others) to whom the state does not have a duty towards.

Foreigners, non-nationals, migrants, refugees, and others are not entitled to certain treatments or privileges that nationals are privy to. This is exacerbated within the Irish Direct Provision system by the abhorrent standards facing people seeking asylum.

In 2004, the Irish government proposed a constitutional amendment which revoked automatic birthright citizenship and allowed them to legislate for citizenship. Excessive scaremongering, such as the then Justice Minister Micheal McDowell's elaborate invention of 'maternity tourism', in which people rush to Ireland to give birth, allowed for the referendum to pass easily, with 79% in favour of the amendment. Children born to non-Irish citizens after 2005 were no longer entitled to Irish citizenship, and were consequently at risk of being rendered stateless.

Citizenship is a key determinant of your ability to live, work, vote and receive an education within Ireland. Individuals now require the favour of the Minister of Justice in exercising discretion in their favour against deportation orders. In 2004, advertisements run by a Fianna Fáil government encouraged voters to "vote yes to common sense citizenship," when perhaps it would have been more relevant to advertise: "vote yes to stateless children."

The exact motives of the Irish government at the time cannot be truly deduced, and the exact effects the clause has had on the lives of the many children born in Ireland cannot be properly quantified – how do we begin to understand the magnitude of uncertainty bound up in being born and raised in a country that refuses to recognise you, to see you as a member of it? While it has the direct effect of stripping children of citizenship and security, it has a more covert effect. The introduction of this clause deliberately prevented the potential issue of Irish citizens being born into Direct Provision.

Irish Citizens could not face the same standards of Direct Provision. No citizen would ever be treated like that at the hands of the state.

It is a quiet but very real admission that we accept differing standards of treatment based on ethnic background, and both the state as well as wider societal norms draw on personal characteristics to justify its treatment of people. The categorisation of distinct but related concepts such as ethnicity, citizenship, and racial identity dictate the material and social privileges we are entitled to within a society, but also influences the way we conceive of (and in turn, treat) ourselves and others.

When the Taliban seized control of Kabul in mid-August, Macron hurried to insist that France and the rest of Europe must protect itself from "waves of migrants." What is it that allows such rhetoric to be socially acceptable? To obscure the lives of individual people in hardship and reduce them to 'waves,' consider them a storm – a threat, is to endorse a fundamental othering of people which surpasses our common conception of race as a description.

Despite our historically interconnected world, and ongoing public commitment to human rights, we insist we owe nothing to those that can be considered beyond our borders. (The seeming irony of this, is of course the urgency at which western powers intervene when deemed geo-politically important. While white saviourism can often expand to accommodate support for interventionism, it is rarely mirrored by support for refugees).

The marriage between "where you are from" and "what you deserve" extends beyond the realms of migrant rights and birthright citizenship – and is strongly related to the movement, confluence and re-invention of ethnic groupings, not just socially but geographically. Cohen (2010), considers the status of 'diaspora.' He notes it can form a powerful "narrative construction," which strategically frames experiences of migration and settlement. As 'diaspora' becomes of political importance in its relationship with legitimate claims to land, it is used more and more frequently. The diaspora term and identity indicate how identity can transcend racial, cultural and local allegiances, and take on a more malleable form.

This is to say that the way we conceptualise ourselves and others goes beyond merely a personal form of self-understanding, and is deeply entangled with the social, cultural and political sphere we occupy. It is worthwhile to ask ourselves: what exactly do these concepts mean? Where did they come from? How do we understand racial and ethnic groupings in such a way as to acknowledge the cultural reality of those around us, while also accommodating for the ever-changing and political nature of racialisation? It is against this backdrop that I began truly speculating the meaning of my own ethnic identity. In short, I decided to ask myself a question that others have been asking me my whole life; where am I really from?

WHAT WE TALK ABOUT WHEN WE TALK ABOUT RACE:
A MIXED RACE CASE STUDY

I've been explaining to people that I am mixed-race my whole life. I've explained it so many times, that I'm not sure if it's information I now actively volunteer, or if I am so used to it being demanded that I offer it instinctively, or preemptively. I've formed a strong connection with the label of mixed-ness itself, while also becoming more confused and worried about the connotations it may hold.

Parker and Song, note that there is a 'persistent myth,' rooted in eighteenth and nineteenth century science, that there were once 'pure' distinct races on earth. This reinforces a view of race as intergenerational and immutable discrete categories. In order to eliminate this worry, it is important to reflect on the very purpose of these labels such as mixed-race.

Mills (1998) in his 'radical constructivist' philosophy, highlights historical racialisation processes that give race socially significant status. Anti-racism must acknowledge the power of the race as a social category and social fact, not through simply seeking to deny its existence. But it must be noted that this discussion of race seeks to replicate and correspond to social realities, not enforce those very concepts of fundamental human difference.

Often, there is a set of beliefs implicit in racial terms, and large amounts of difficulties involved in categorising people within racial groups in such a way as to both reject unscientific notions of race-science and reflect their social realities.

Developing questions around ethnic and racial identity for official use (such as in census data, medical data or diversity reports) is particularly difficult. Owen (2001) notes that statisticians have trouble designing questions around ethnic origin as by presenting mutually exclusive boxes, each containing discrete categories of race, one presents the idea that there is a set of 'real' ethnic categories beyond that of societal norms, and that every person belongs to one of these groups – or at least, should belong to one of these groups.

Neither should classification and categorisation be seen as value-free processes. This much is demonstrated by empirical research, such as that of Martin Bulmer (1986). Bulmer analyses the changes in terminology used by researchers in major studies between 1948 and 1983, which demonstrates obvious shifts in classifications over time, (from categories such as 'negro' to 'coloured' etc.). Owen (2001) further notes that the inclusion of mixed-race people in the British Census was in part due to consultations findings that mixed-race people were often happy and eager to describe themselves as such. These findings contrasted strongly with previous studies which suggested unhappy and painful identities plagued mixed-race people, and posed severe challenges for ideals built on segregation or white purity.

The sociological concept of the 'Marginal Man' gained popularity in the USA. Marginal Man theory contended that a mixed-race person would perpetually be caught between two distinct and different cultural realities and would hence be unable to establish a sense of identity (Stonequist, 1937).

Other influential US studies such as that of Reuter (1918) claimed 'the mulatto' was prone to outbursts and frustration. It is clear that the 'marginal man' which Stonequist speaks of, "never acts but overreacts" (Furedi 2001). Stonequist (1937) depicts the 'marginal man' as hypersensitive, as one who finds incidents of discrimination and racism where none was intended, or who forces a racialised views on the world. This historical view of mixed-race people as inherently problematic and unhappy supported the case for segregation in both the USA and Britain.

Segregation was claimed to be a personal preference and segregationists insisted that people did not desire to mix (Furedi, 2001). More than that, the deep unhappiness and agitation of a mixed-race person is necessary in order to frame anti-racist politics supported by mixed-race people as an unhappy person's methods of acquiring self-esteem rather than a legitimate socio-political grievance (Furedi 2001). Thus, it appears the first challenge to any data being gathered on mixed-race individuals is for there to be a legitimate will to gather it.

Fears surrounding race-mixing existed in both the US and Britain. In the US, it was predominantly driven to preserve 'white prestige' while in Britain, fears around race-mixing formed the backbone of a strict 'code of breeding' which preserved race and class status (Furedi 2001). The political nature of race studies and the divergence in such data can be explained by the changing and evolving nature of race politics within a region.

My relationship with mixed-ness becomes further complicated when considering my personal lack of connection to my Indian heritage. I have no contact with the Indian side of my family and so, what even makes me mixed, apart from the alienation and rejection that I face from my white peers? Have I been assigned this identity purely by others? If so, why?

When I decide to call myself mixed-race, I feel powerful – like I am positively associating myself with a label that so many see as a form of personal tragedy, of loss, or of animalism. And yet, I know it is my Irishness, my proximity to whiteness, my citizenship, my hold on the English language, my access to resources, that determines all of the privileges I have access to. Why is it that so much of our lives are determined by these arbitrary characteristics?

Conclusion

This essay barely scratches the surface of race and racialisation, and hardly begins to explore the wide array of injustices faced by BIPOC communities across the world. What I hoped to illustrate was simply that there is deep-rooted and complex social baggage associated with the assignment of racial, ethnic, and ultimately, citizenship statuses.

The assignment of such categories are confused and riddled with political and social agendas, and it is better to look at these categories as moving constructs, rather than innate immutable forces.

Ultimately, this essay raises more questions than it answers, but it is nonetheless part of a wider project which asks: who decides who we are, and who decides what we get?

Gabrielle Fullam

Gabrielle is an Irish-Punjabi writer and theatre-maker living in Dublin. She is author of *Hands And Knees* newsletter, and Editor of *Icarus* magazine. She is a Political Science, Philosophy, Economics and Sociology student at Trinity College Dublin, where she is also a Laidlaw Foundation Research Scholar. Her research focuses on mixed-race experience and identity, centring the experience of mixed race people, and questioning the boundaries of racialised categories.

Gabrielle Recommends:

BOOKS

Lost Children Archive by Valeria Luiselli,

Embroideries by Marjane Satrapi

A Feather on the Breath of God by Singred Nunez

Black Skin, White Masks by Frantz Fanon

Racial Formation in the United States by Micheal Omi and Howard Winant

TELEVISION/DOCUMENTARIES

Matangi/MAYA/M.I.A.

I May Destroy You.

White Delusion

White delusion. It is dangerous, it is idle, it is defensive and most importantly, it is why racism and white supremacy run rampant today.

Marcia Gunn

On December 30th 2020, George Nkencho was shot in the back six times and killed by Gardaí. While his family were inside, he was shot several times in front of their home in Dublin. This occurred after George assaulted a man in a convenience store while holding a knife. George Nkencho suffered from mental health issues and, despite a spread of misinformation following his death, had no criminal convictions.

When George Floyd was killed by police in America in May 2020, lots of Irish people claimed that racism does not exist in Ireland and that racism is a problem for the United States of America and the United Kingdom. This is white delusion at its finest. To think that any Western society does not operate under white supremacy is delusional and false.

White delusion has deceived white people into thinking that racism is a thing of the past, occurs in isolated incidents and is never present in their lives. Neither case was the first time that the authority figures that were meant to protect and serve a nation failed to do so, yet lots of white people operate under the lie that both murders were not racially motivated and not part of the systematic oppression that is racism.

Both cases see race be a motivating factor in their murder because there have been incidents in which white people have committed worse crimes and have not been killed for doing so and instead were given compassion and a light punishment.

An example of this would be when Trump supporters stormed Capitol Hill on January 6th and assaulted police and members of Congress. Very few were even arrested and none were beaten or killed. This is in stark contrast to how the police treated Black Lives Matter (BLM) protesters in 2020 as they were beaten, arrested and assaulted with tear gas.

Two major differences in these examples are obvious. BLM protesters were peacefully protesting against the systematic injustice that has plagued Black people for several centuries and their cries for humanity were met with violence. Trump supporters however, committed domestic terrorism because they refused to accept the result of a fair democratic election, yet it was the BLM protesters (the majority of which were black) who were met with violence. All these incidents show how authority figures view the mere presence of Black people as threatening and irrationally respond to us with violence, while violent white people are treated as if they are victims. Not acknowledging this is white delusion and that is a major factor in why white supremacy runs rampant in all Western societies today.

White delusion manifests in different ways. Another example came from a white male friend of mine. Shortly after Joe Biden and Kamala Harris had won the 2020 US Presidential Election, my friend expressed his hopes for four years' time, where Harris would be able to run on her own for the next Presidential Election. On the surface, this seems like a wonderful statement as he is overtly supporting the idea of a Black and Asian woman leading the most influential and powerful country in the world.

Here is the delusion: America has been terrorised by Trump, his administration and his followers since 2016 and 74+ million people still voted for him in the 2020 Election. Therefore, why would anyone think that a massive portion of American citizens are going to wake up in 2024, suddenly not be racist, and vote for a Black and Asian woman to run their country? Keep in mind that many Black people were brutally murdered by the police in 2020 (like many other years proceeding), were tear gassed and shot at by the police and that Asians were blamed for the COVID-19 pandemic and suffered numerous hate crimes. I ask again, how could Kamala Harris being elected President in 2024 be plausible?

Make no mistake about it, I want Black women to aspire for whatever they want and to get everything that we deserve. For too long, we have been pushed aside, dismissed and used for others, who are less qualified and more privileged, to get ahead.

What I am saying is that for my friend, and many other white people, thinking the above situation is plausible, is in fact delusional, naï ve and foolish. It shows that they are not fully engaged with reality because if they were, they would know that nothing about the white supremacist societies that exist in the Western world suggest that this is plausible.

This is because Western societies still operate under the lie that white people, particularly white men, are the only ones deserving of power, peace and happiness and other races need to, at worst, be exterminated, and at best, exist to serve white people.

By believing that the United States of America would wake up in four years' time and not be racist, despite modern day America being built off racism and white supremacy through them enslaving Africans and committing genocide against Native American people, he fails to acknowledge the real experiences and effects that white supremacy has on people of colour.

On another occasion, the same friend went on to say that destroying white supremacy is a "mammoth task" and he feels like "there's only so much he can do as one insignificant person." Yes, this man actually said this to me; a black woman.

Readers, please do not take this as an isolated attack on this one person, as lots of white people think this way. White delusion allows white people to not fully engage in reality, or like the last example, somehow centre themselves in the destruction of racism and white supremacy. When people of colour say that racism is a problem for white people to solve, we do not mean that it is on the shoulders of one white individual to clean up.

What we mean (and I thought that with all the resources and it being 2021 that this would be clear now) is that racism was invented by white people to hurt and destroy other races. Therefore, as they made this mess, it is up to them to clean up. This is because white people benefit the most from racism but are also hurt by it, just not to the extent that other races are.

Due to us living in white supremacist societies, white people will have the loudest voices when encountering racism. A disturbing fact but it is the sad truth. By that I mean, if a white person says something racist and me, a black woman, opposes it, the racist will disregard what I say, as they do not see me as equal and expect the opposition.

However, if a white person opposes it, then the racist will be jarred, surprised and could change their views depending on how deeply committed they are to being a bigot. This is the bare minimum that white people are expected to do to dismantle white supremacy.

What an anti-racist society needs white people to do, is to continue learning and putting what they have learned into practice. It is not enough for them to read some Langston Hughes poems and to like Beyoncé. They must be engaged in reality, they have to actively combat racism at all times and they have to confront their white delusion with full force every single day. If not, we will continue to die at the hands of their negligence. We have lost way too many that way and we do not deserve to lose any more. White people need to DO BETTER or continue to uphold the systems you claim to not to be a part of.

PERFORMATIVE ACTIVISM
Understanding the harm performative activism causes to the communities that people claim they are trying to aid

Ashley Chadamoyo Makombe

While over the years social media has been considered an extremely useful tool for activists, and NGOs to gather attention for their causes, the subsequent lockdown in 2020 and the 24-hour news cycle made social media the modern-day activists most useful tool. With the death of George Floyd, the annexation of Palestine, the end SARS movement and countless other world events and human rights violations, one of the biggest things to come out of it, is the birth of the social media activism, in which everyday individuals use their own platforms, regardless of how big or small they may be, in order to spread awareness of the treatment of others across the globe.

On the surface, this can seem beneficial. Opening up Instagram or Twitter to see everyone discussing the latest political news and giving a voice to those that may not have could be seen as a good thing. But there are multiple issues with the growth of social media activism, and most of them would end up fitting into the category of Performative Activism.

Performative Activism can best be described as, well, performing. It is the act of sharing news in order to seem cool and woke to your friends and followers, rather than doing it for the genuine care of the people affected by the issue that you are discussing. And while there is a strong argument in favour of performative activism as many would say it still raises awareness of sensitive world issues, the harm performative activism causes to the communities that people claim they are trying to aid is greater than it may seem.

Activism as its core must uplift those who face the issue directly. Oftentimes performative activism can end up with people centering themselves in an issue that has nothing to do with them, rather than promoting the experts/victims of the issue. For example, this past summer when the news of the annexation of Palestinians from their homes by the Israeli government made its way into the mainstream, many Irish people all over Twitter shared a map that showed what it would like if Ireland lost the same amount of land the Palestinians had.

While at first glance it can seem like a good, simplified way for people to understand the gravity of the situation and relate it to home, the action can be seen as performative activism. Rather than sharing resources and explanations by Palestinian refugees or activists or reporters, the map centred Irishness in a conversation that had little to do with them. It was to the detriment to Palestinians as well as Irish people as, depending on who you ask, Ireland still has part of the land stolen from them. By centring Ireland and Irishness on an issue that has nothing to do with the country, it took away from an amazing opportunity to highlight and uplift Palestinian voices.

In a society that centres narratives that are very often cisgendered, straight, white male-dominated, it can be hard to recognize your own actions as being rooted in performative activism. A lot of the time what we consider activism charity in the western world once fully analysed is a form of performative activism.

For example, the Habitat for Humanity trip that you took during TY on the surface looks like a charitable thing to do. Once you begin to decenter whiteness and privilege from your day to day you soon realise how patronising the idea of sending twenty odd unqualified European students to a 'developing country' to build houses is when there are qualified builders in that country that may just lack the resources to help themselves.

It's almost impossible to tackle the topic of performative activism without bringing up its big sister, white saviorism, as the two are intrinsically linked. One of the largest issues surrounding performative activism is the centring of white narratives around world issues. For decades, white people have placed themselves as 'the cure' for decades-long institutionalised inequality (which they caused) in developing countries. Even the term 'developing' when describing these places is disingenuous as the inequality in those countries is as a result of overexploitation by the same institutions that claim to help them.

While the issue of performative activism has been exasperated by the use of social media, it is by no means a new phenomenon. In 1998, Barbra Green published a novel titled, *Spectacular Confessions: Autobiography, Performative Activism, and the Sites of Suffrage*, which was about women's suffrage in Australia during the federation era. Since the beginning of freedom and liberation movements, performative activism has been an issue.

The concept of performative activism and the feelings of white privilege/guilt cannot be separated. In the age of social media, the fear of cancel culture (which may not even exist), has led many people to worry more and more about their reputation being tarnished rather than world issues. This leads to many people feeling pressured to share certain posts and news stories in an attempt to look informed and caring to their audience, whether that audience be hundreds of thousands of strangers just their close friends and family.

The issue with pretending to care about certain world topics in order to protect your image is that no genuine change can be made from that. Yes, posting black squares on Instagram and sharing Twitter threads and infographics can be a great start in your personal activism journey but those actions are just that, the start. If you don't show up to vote, come to protests or even donate money and resources when and if you can, your support begins and ends on the internet.

But people's lives aren't on the internet. People aren't internet trends but when you reduce someone's life down to a hashtag on a t-shirt or an aesthetically pleasing graphic on Instagram you reduce the gravity of the situation, and after two or three weeks, maybe a month if you're lucky, they become old news and whatever happened to that person or that place or that group of people is completely forgotten about.

This is not to say that you shouldn't share those posts on your social media platforms. It just means that with everything you must remember that there are real people being affected by these issues. When posting something ask yourself, "Am I doing it because I want to?" When you place the needs of others above the fear of your reputation you stop performing, and you start being a real ally.

Ashley Chadamoyo Makombe

Ashley is a writer and producer, and is currently a 3rd-year journalism student at the Technological University Dublin. She is also the Co-Founder of *The GALPAL Collective*, an arts and media collective dedicated to the celebration, creation, curation and support of works by young queer folk, women, and people of colour. Her background in music and theatre and love of pop culture has a large influence on how she creates, and as a writer and producer, Ashley's work typically centres around what it means to be a young black woman in Ireland.

Ashley Recommends:

BOOKS

Women, Race and Class by Angela Davis,

On Intersectionality: Essential Writings by Kimberlé Williams Crenshaw

OTHER MEDIA

The Problem of Performative Activism, AlJazeera News, 20 July 2020 https://www.aljazeera.com/opinions/2020/7/20/the-problem-of-performative-activism

Dear White People (TV show)

The Patriot Act starring Hassan Minhaj

See more of Ashley's work:

TWITTER & INSTAGRAM - @ashleychadamoyo

WEBSITE - www.thegalpalcollective.com

LIFE AFTER HOSTELS
Navigating the ambiguity of leaving the Direct Provision system and settling into the complexity of a new system

Diane Ihirwe

Direct Provision is like the overprotective, overbearing step-parent we watch in scary movies and read in grim novels. They give you the bare minimum to maintain their outward image because they profit from your presence in the house. They give you just enough to keep you alive and happy for the public and for self-serving reasons, but providing you with adequate care is a farfetched concept. Their abuse is calculated and hidden, so much so that outsiders think they are doing their very best because if you don't like it there you can always go back to your mother's house; where you came from.

Three years ago, I got a call from a mother who had recently gotten her 'papers.' She called me in a panic wondering what the noise was in her house. She thought it was the fire alarm, but her appliances and electricity were off, and it was only coming from her place. She lived in an apartment block so she was worried that her neighbours were listening and judging her. In her mind, there was a possibility that they would call the Department of Justice and her papers would be revoked. As if it was written on her forehead that she was coming from a Direct Provision Centre and as if everyone has the number of the Department of Justice on speed dial.

You see, in the Direct Provision system, fear is a weapon utilised to silence those who speak up. Managers, cleaners and even those who are supposed to feed you, know they have power over you. The power imbalance and power struggle manifests itself through scare-mongering techniques of "I'll call Justice."

This statement is often thrown around as if 'Justice' is the ubiquitous uncle of every staff member in the Centres. This mentality is ingrained in people's psyche so much that they think any small mistake, misunderstanding or disagreement might result in the other party calling Justice on them. Continuing on, my friend was apologetic because she felt embarrassed to ask me "such a silly question" yet inconsolable because she had no clue what the noise was, and she thought she had broken the house and might consequently be deported.

My friend was in her 40s, she had three children and had lived in Ireland for nine years. All her time in Ireland was spent in a Direct Provision Centre. She often put it into perspective and said, "I spent 3,294 days in a single room with three growing children."

Lentin (2016) ascertains that the Direct Provision System was created to "isolate people seeking asylum in a child-parent-like relationship where they receive food and shelter and subsequently depend on the State." The only difference with a normal child-parent-relationship is that this particular parent doesn't prepare the children for the outside; the Big Bad World. The world with no centre manager. The world where people don't have to constantly survive on the mercy of strangers. The world where you don't have to queue for food. The world where the manager won't call Justice because you asked for the second roll of toilet paper in a row. The world where a choice of washing machines, kettle and service providers are as difficult as what schools your kids might attend. Because one of the biggest human right infringements within the walls of Direct Provision centres, is lack of choice.

You will never understand the importance of choice until, every night at 7pm, you have to queue up for rice and chicken; the only dinner available to you. And if you happen to be elsewhere, you will go hungry with no questions asked. You will never understand the importance of choice until you have to ration toilet paper and baby milk. Because, if you don't ration them, the centre manager will shame you in front of everyone, saying that you use too much toilet paper and that your baby is too hungry and will get fat. You will never understand the importance of choice, until a bathroom sink, shared with another single parent, is the only sterilised surface available to wash your baby's bottles. You will never understand the importance of choice, until your child is unwell with a vomiting bug, yet they have to go to bed hungry because they don't want to eat rice for the consecutive 3,280th day, but you can't afford what they want or simply don't have access to a shop. You will never understand choice, until children as old as seven have no capacity to make a choice, because they've never had a choice before. You will never understand the importance of choice, until you have none. You will never understand the importance of choice, until choices become alien to you.

After four, five, ten years in Direct Provision, a choice becomes an unattainable wish. The word choice is non-existent in your vocabulary, so much that you imagine other people don't have choices either.

However, thankfully and suddenly, the papers come, and you get to have a choice. But how do you make a choice when you've never had to? How do you make a choice when you don't know how that's done? Something as simple as a choice becomes such a heavy burden to bear, because suddenly, it is a vital factor to navigate life within the new societal system.

But, unlike the old system where you woke up, ate, slept and waited for the brown envelope protecting your papers to arrive; the new system has rules and regulations, with managers that aren't constantly there. These rules and regulations differ from those in your old system, in that they are important for you to maintain your papers, but they are complicated and often difficult to navigate alone. And so, the sudden choices you are given are accompanied by layers of complexity.

Bureaucracy, laws, regulations, norms, values and standards of conformity. These layers did not apply in the old system and no one explained that they were needed in the new societal system. No one prepared you for them. No one prepared you to live in the new system, but everyone expects that now you've got your papers you must get out, get a job, pay back the system that put up with you, don't be a sponger and a scrounger, don't moan, and most of all, speak good English or else go back to where you came from.

Don't forget that before you do all of this, you must adhere to the systems in place. You must know and understand them even though no one explained them to you. Suddenly, you can choose where to live but no, you actually can't! Because you need to have connections in whatever place you choose to live. Suddenly, you have a choice of going to education. But wait! You must have certain types of papers. Suddenly, you can have a home. But wait! We need three previous references from landlords. Suddenly, you have a home and all the appliances within to make a perfect meal for your family. But wait! You have no idea how any of them work. You've forgotten how to cook. You must choose a provider suited to your needs and within your budget. Suddenly, you can open up a bank account and apply for a driving license. But wait! We need proof of address and a GNIB card; social welfare cards aren't sufficient. Suddenly, you have a choice! But soon after, you realise that a choice with no support is a choice in vain. A choice within a system you can't navigate is not a choice after all. In certain circumstances, equality oppresses the vulnerable therefore equity should be the goal.

Although both equality and equity promote and strive for fairness, the difference between the two must be emphasised. Equality strives for reaching fairness by treating everyone the same "regardless of needs" while equity achieves fairness by treating people differently "depending on their needs" (Fantini, 1988). Equity should be the aim. Intersections and complexity of life should be at the core of decision-making processes to ensure no one is falling through the cracks of bureaucracy. Decisions made to support people in the Direct Provision System and beyond, should be evaluated through an equity framework, not necessarily equality, to ensure everyone's needs are met.

Direct Provision has a myriad of disadvantages, but one of the best things about being idle with plenty of restrictions is the appreciation of the little things. Appreciation of people, friendships created and family. The friendships, camaraderie and family-like relationships formed within the walls of Direct Provision Centres are by far my favourite memory of life in hostels, hotels, unaccompanied minors' rooms, homework corners and at dining tables. Shared trauma has a way of uniting people.

The commonalities found, in waiting for that brown envelope, the English classes, the queuing for food and asking for yet another soap, is a beautiful yet unexplainable bond that sustains people within the system and beyond.

Life after Direct Provision isn't all rosy. But resilience and strength-based parenting styles, prevalent in most third world countries, keep asylum seekers afloat. Practices and beliefs of focussing on the positive, religious beliefs, spirituality and connections made within Direct Provision Centres are pillars to sustaining people within the system and beyond. However, just because asylum seekers might manage well after leaving the system, doesn't mean that the system is working, nor that it is best practice.

The government should prepare asylum seekers for life after the system. They should be prepared to navigate the complexity of the new system. They should be supported within the system and beyond, because navigating the complexity of the structures of a new societal system requires support that should be offered when people are still in the previous system. Releasing people in an unknown world with no support is setting them up for failure.

If prisoners, care leavers, and people within communal homeless accommodations and others living within communal accommodations can be supported to navigate the new systems, why can't asylum seekers? Accommodation can be supported to navigate the new systems, why can't asylum seekers?

I have worked in domestic violence, homelessness, with children in the care system and with asylum seekers. And there is a visible difference in how people are treated and expected to navigate the new world. Asylum seekers bear the brunt of it. They are expected to understand and know it all. To prepare them to live in a world that often operates in a different sequence that they are used to. Preparing them to live in the new society will equip them with tools, knowledge and confidence to navigate the complexity of the new world on the other side of Direct Provision.

Diane Ihirwe

Diane is an African-Irish social worker, speaker , writer and social justice seeker. She is a graduate of Master in Social Work from Trinity College and holds an undergraduate degree in Social Care from TU Dublin. Diane speaks about racism from everyday life, as well as systemic and structural racism and its impact . She advocates for the abolition of the Direct Provision System. She travelled to the United Nations (UN) in Geneva in December 2019 to advocate on behalf of Asylum Seekers on the Committee of Eradicating Racial Discrimination (CERD). In 2014, Diane co-founded the Young Mother's Network (YMN), a support group for mothers living in Direct Provision Centres. Diane is the co-Founder of Rooted In Africa and Ireland Network (RIAINetwork), a network that aims to build understanding and pride of the African Heritage especially for young African-Irish people through knowledge, empowerment and representation.

Diane Recommends:

BOOKS

Skin Like Mine by Lateshia M. Perry

The Proudest Bleu by Ibtihaj Muhammad and S.K. Ali

Hair Love by Mathew Cherry

The Fire Next Time by James Baldwin

Natives: Race and Class in the Ruins of Empire by Alaka

Why Are All the Black Kids Sitting Together in the Cafeteria? by Beverly Daniel Totum, PhD

See more of Diane's Work:

WEBSITE - www.riainetwork.com

INSTAGRAM - @diane_ihirwe / @riainetwork

TWITTER - @Diane_Ihirwe / @riainetwork

254

Artwork

Kaiser Caimo

Page - "this place is a jungle" ; history and politics chapter page; 50; 51; 53;

See more: caisercaimo.com

Teresa Colfer

Page - 60; 62

see more:

    instagram - @tmecolfer / teresacolferartist

Shannon Keegan

Page - introduction title page; 46; 55; 254; back cover

see more:

    instagram - @shannonkeeganart

Ciara Leneghan-White

Page - 211

See more:

    instagram - @eekywyke

Artwork

Annie Mar

Page - 212

See more:

    instagram - @an_na_mar

Barry Quinn

Page - front cover; spine; inner page; v; 48; the notes chapter page; 191; 257; end

See more: barryquinn.ie

    instagram - @barryquinnart twitter - @barryquinnart

Katrīna Tračuma

Page - 216

See more: katrinatracuma.com

    instagram - @akissforkatart

    youtube - a kiss for kat

    facebook - katrina tracuma art

Anastasiia zubareva

Page - the lives title page; 58

See more:

    instagram - @lis_a.Rt.Z

BIBLIOGRAPHY

Alagha, Y., 2021. *Genocide, but make it feminist: The cultural genocide of the Uighurs.* [online] Rogue Collective, July 10th 2021. Available at: <www.roguecollective.ie>.

Bulmer, M., 1986. 'Race and Ethnicity.' In R.G. Burgess (ed.), *Key Variables in Social Investigation.* London: Routledge.

Bracken-Roche, D., Bell, E., Macdonald, M.E. and Racine, E., 2017. *The concept of 'vulnerability' in research ethics: an in-depth analysis of policies and guidelines. Health research policy and systems, 15*(1), p.8.

Breen, C., 2008. The policy of Direct Provision in Ireland: a violation of asylum seekers' right to an adequate standard of housing. *International Journal of Refugee Law, 20*(4), pp.611-636.

Cannon, T., 1994. Vulnerability analysis and the explanation of 'natural' disasters. *Disasters, Development and Environment,* 1, pp.13-30.

Carr, H. and Lipscomb, S., 2021. *What is History, Now?.* London: Orion Publishing.

Carswell, S., 2014. *Shannon played vital logistical role in rendition circuits, say researchers.* [online] The Irish Times, December 9th 2014.

Charles, M. and Bellinson, J., 2019. *The Importance of Play in Early Childhood Education.* London: Taylor and Francis.

Children's Rights., 2020. [online] Available at: <www.childrensrights.ie>.

Christie, J. F., & Johnsen, E. P., 1983. The role of play in social-intellectual development. *Review of Educational Research, 53*(1), pp.93-115.

Citizensinformation.ie, 2021. *Direct Provision system.* [online] Available at: <www.citizensinformation.ie/en/moving_country/ asylum_seekers_and_refugees/services_for_asylum_seekers_in_ireland/ direct_provision.html > [Accessed September 21, 2021].

College of Psychiatrists Ireland (CPI)., 2017. *The Mental Health Service Requirements in Ireland for Asylum Seekers, Refugees and Migrants from Conflict Zones.* [online] Available at: <www.irishpsychiatry.ie>.

Cohen, P., 2010. Rethinking the Diasporama. *Patterns of Prejudice, 33*(1), pp. 3-22.

Connolly, L., 2019. Honest Commemoration: Reconciling Women's Troubled and Troubling History in Centennial Ireland. *MUSSI Working Paper Series No-9*: Maynooth University Social Sciences Institute.

Creasey, G. L., Jarvis, P. A., & Berk, L. E., 1998. Play and social competence. In O. N. Saracho & B. Spodek (eds.), *Multiple perspectives on play in early childhood education*. New York: State University of New York Press, pp. 116–143

Crowley, U. and Kitchin, R., 2008. Producing 'decent girls': governmentality and the moral geographies of sexual conduct in Ireland (1922–1937). *Gender, Place & Culture, 15*(4), pp.358-372.

Crumlish, N. and Bracken, P., 2011. Mental health and the asylum process. *Irish Journal of Psychological Medicine*, 28(2), pp.57-60.

Dabiri, E., 2021. *What White People Can Do Next*. London: Penguin Books.

Delor, F. and Hubert, M., 2000. Revisiting the concept of 'vulnerability'. *Social Science & Medicine*, 50(11), pp.1557-1570.

Doras, 2020. *Direct Provision*. [online] Available at: <doras.org>.

Doras, 2020. *Mental Health and Direct Provision: Recommendations for Addressing Urgent Concerns*. [online] Available at: <doras.org>.

Fáilte Ireland, 2018. *Key Tourism Facts 2018*. [online] Available at: <www.failteireland.ie>.

Furedi, F., 2001. 'How sociology imagined race mixing.' In Parker, D. & Song, M. (eds.), *Rethinking 'Mixed Race'*. London: Pluto Press.

Enright, M., 2017. 'Involuntary Patriotism: Judgement, Women and the National Identity on the Island of Ireland.' In M. Enright, McCandless, J. and O'Donoghue, A. (eds.), *Northern/Irish Feminist Judgements: Judges' Troubles and the Gendered Politics of Identity*. Oxford: Hart Publishing, pp.27-49.

European Web Site on Integration., 2021. *Getting right to work: Access to employment and decent work for international protection applicants in Ireland*. [online] Available at: <www.ec.europa.eu>.

Erickson, R. J., 1985. 'Play contributes to the full emotional development of the child.' *Education, 105*(3).

Fanning, B., & Veale, A., 2004. 'Child poverty as public policy: Direct Provision and asylum seeker children in the Republic of Ireland.' *Child Care in Practice, 10*(3), pp.241-251.

Fantini, M., 1988. 'Changing Conceptions of Equality'. *Equity & Excellence in Education*, 24(2), pp.21-23.

Finnegan, M. and O'Donoghue, B., 2017. Rethinking vulnerable groups in clinical research. *Irish Journal of Psychological Medicine*, pp.1-9.

Gallen, J., 2019. 'Gender and Politics.' In Black, L. and Dunne, P. (eds.), *Law and Gender in Modern Ireland: Critique and Reform*. Oxford: Hart Publishing.

Gartland, F., 2014. Ireland 'complicit' in CIA torture by failing to search flights. [online] The Irish Times. December 13th 2014. Available at: <www.irishtimes.com>.

Gusciute, E., 2020. Leaving the most vulnerable behind: Reflection on the Covid-19 pandemic and Direct Provision in Ireland. *Irish Journal of Sociology, 28*(2), pp.237-241.

Graham, A.M., 2012. *Unmarried Mothers: The Legislative Context in Ireland 1921-1979*. Department of History: NUI Maynooth.

Glaser, E., 2021. *Motherhood: A Manifesto*. London: Harper Collins.

Goek, S., 2015. *From Ireland to the US: a brief migration history*. [online] The Irish Times, October 29th 2015. Available at: <irishtimes.com>.

Hill, M., Campanale, D. and Gunter, J., 2021. *'Their goal is to destroy everyone': Uighur camp detainees allege systematic rape*. [online] BBC News, Februay 2nd 2021. Available at: <www.bbc.com>.

Hilliard, M., 2019. *Direct Provision in Ireland: How and why the system was introduced*. [online] The Irish Times, November 19th 2019. Available at: <http://www.irishtimes.com>

Horgan, G., 2001. Changing Women's Lives in Ireland. *International Socialism Journal, 91*.

Howard, J., & McInnes, K., 2013. 'The impact of children's perception of an activity as play rather than not play on emotional well-being.' *Child: Care, Health and Development, 39*(5), pp.737-742.

Irish Refugee Council, 2011. *Direct Provision and Dispersal: Is there an alternative?*. [online] Dublin: NGO Forum on Direct Provision. Available at: <www.irishrefugeecouncil.ie>.

Justice.ie. 2021. *Minister McEntee announces reduced 6 month waiting period for international protection applicants to access work - The Department of Justice*. [online] January 28th 2021. Available at: <http://www.justice.ie>.

Karlsson, S., 2018. 'Do you know what we do when we want to play?" Children's hidden politics of resistance and struggle for play in a Swedish asylum centre.' *Childhood*, 25(3), pp.311–324.

Karatekin, C., 2018. Adverse childhood experiences (ACEs), stress and mental health in college students. *Stress and Health, 34*(1), pp.36-45.

Keena, C., 2019. *China Cables: 'The largest incarceration of a minority since the Holocaust'.* [online] The Irish Times, November 24th 2019. Available at: <www.irishtimes.com> .

Kenny, A., 2021. *Asylum seekers' difficulty finding work over 'unconvincing permits'.* [online] The Irish Times, March 22nd 2021 Available at: <www.irishtimes.com>.

Lee, M., 2021. *Asylum seeker fears death as hunger strike enters eighth day.* [online] Irish Examiner, October 20th 2021. Available at: <www.irishexaminer.com>.

Lentin, R. (2016). Asylum seekers, Ireland, and the return of the repressed. *Irish Studies Review, 24*(1), pp.21-34.

Lustig, S. L. *et al.*, 2004. Review of child and adolescent refugee mental health. *Journal of the American Academy of Child & Adolescent Psychiatry, 43*(1), pp.24-36.

MASI, 2021. *Statement on White Paper to end Direct Provision.* [Online] February 29th 2021. Available at: <www. masi.ie>.

McMahon, J. D., Macfarlane, A., Avalos, G. E., et al., 2007. A survey of asylum seekers' general practice service utilisation and morbidity patterns. *Irish Medical Journal, 100,* pp.461–464

McVane, B., 2020. PTSD in asylum-seekers: Manifestations and relevance to the asylum process. *Psychiatry Research*, 284.

Nath, S., and Szücs, D., 2014. Construction play and cognitive skills associated with the development of mathematical abilities in 7-year-old children. *Learning and Instruction*, 32, pp.73-80.

Nijhof, S. L. et al., 2018. Healthy play, better coping: The importance of play for the development of children in health and disease. *Neuroscience & Biobehavioral Reviews, 95*, pp.421-429.

Nestor, O., & Moser, C. S. (2018). The importance of play. *Journal of Occupational Therapy, Schools, & Early Intervention, 11*(3), 247-262.

O'Connell, M., Duffy, R., & Crumlish, N. (2016). Refugees, the asylum system and mental healthcare in Ireland. B*JPsych. International, 13*(02), pp.35–37.

O'Connor, D., O'Rourke, V., Robinson McGunnigle, C., & McCormack, M., 2017. The influences of opportunity. Differences in children's play choices across diverse communities in Ireland. *INTED 2017 Valencia*: IATED Academy.

O'Doherty, C., 2021. *Ghost estates: Thousands of homeowners in fight to get ghost estates completed.* [online] Independent, July 10th 2021. Available at: <www.independent.ie>.

O'Reilly, Z., 2019. The Politics and Practice of Exclusion. *The In-Between Spaces of Asylum and Migration*, pp.57-94.

O'Reilly, Z., 2018. 'Living Liminality': everyday experiences of asylum seekers in the 'Direct Provision' system in Ireland. *Gender, Place & Culture, 25*(6), pp.821-842.

O'Rourke, M., 2011. Recommendation to Ireland Regarding the Magdalene Laundries. *Concluding Observations of the United Nations Committee against Torture*, p.1.

O'Rourke, M., 2017. Justice for Magdalene Report. *NGO Submission to the UN Committee Against Torture*.

Owen, C., 2001. 'Mixed Race' in Official Statistics. In Parker D. & Song M. (eds.), *Rethinking 'Mixed Race'*. London: Pluto Press, pp.134-153.

Park, A. T. et al., 2018. Amygdala–medial prefrontal cortex connectivity relates to stress and mental health in early childhood. *Social Cognitive and Affective Neuroscience, 13*(4), pp.430-439.

Parker, D. and Song, M., 2001. 'Introduction: Rethinking 'Mixed Race'.' In Parker D. & Song M. (eds.), *Rethinking 'Mixed Race.'* London: Pluto Press, pp.1-22.

Pedersen, D., 2002. Political violence, ethnic conflict, and contemporary wars: broad implications for health and social well-being. *Social Science & Medicine, 55*(2), pp.175-190.

Pinto Wiese, E. B., & Burhorst, I., 2007. The mental health of asylum-seeking and refugee children and adolescents attending a clinic in the Netherlands. *Transcultural Psychiatry, 44*(4), pp.596-613.

Pollak, S., 2019. *Asylum seeker weekly allowance rises for adults and children.* [online] The

Irish Times, March 25ᵗʰ 2019. Available at: <www.irishtimes.com>.

Psychological Society of Ireland, 2020. *Impact of COVID-19 on mental health.* [online] Available at: <www.psychologicalsociety.ie>.

Reception and Integration Agency, 2018. *Monthly Report October 2018.* [online] Department of Justice and Equality, pp.2 - 7. Available at: <www.ria.gov.ie>.

Reception and Integration Agency, 2019. Department of Justice and Equality, *RIA: Background.* [online] Available at: <www.ria.gov.ie>

Reuter, E.B., 1918. *The Mulatto in the United States.* Boston: Scribner

Robinson, M., 2021. *Cherising the Irish Diaspora | President of Ireland.* [online] February 2ⁿᵈ 1995. Available at: <www.president.ie>.

Ryan, D.A., Benson, C.A. and Dooley, B.A., 2008. Psychological distress and the asylum process: A longitudinal study of forced migrants in Ireland. *The Journal of Nervous and Mental Disease*, 196(1), pp.37-45.

Ryan, D.A., Kelly, F.E. and Kelly, B.D., 2009. Mental health among persons awaiting an asylum outcome in Western countries: A literature review. *International Journal of Mental Health*, 38(3), pp.88-111.

Said, E., 1978. *Orientalism.* New York, NY: Penguin Books.

Seanad Éireann, 1955. *Factories Bill.* Committee 11 May, Seanad Éireann Debate, 44(15).

Sanchez-Cao, E., Kramer, T., & Hodes, M. (2013). Psychological distress and mental health service contact of unaccompanied asylum-seeking children. *Child: Care, Health and Development, 39*(5), pp.651-659.

Seja, A. L., & Russ, S. W., 1999. Children's fantasy play and emotional understanding. *Journal of Clinical Child Psychology, 28*(2), pp.269–277.

Shah, K. and Adolphe, J., 2019. *400 years since slavery: a timeline of American history.* [online] The Guardian, August 16ᵗʰ 2019. Available at: <www.theguardian.com>.

Silove, D., Sinnerbrink, I., Field, A., Manicavasagar, V. and Steel, Z., 1997. Anxiety, depression and PTSD in asylum-seekers: associations with pre-migration trauma and post-migration stressors. *The British Journal of Psychiatry*, *170*(4), pp.351-357.

Silove, D., Steel, Z. and Watters, C., 2000. Policies of deterrence and the mental health of asylum seekers. *Jama*, *284*(5), pp.604-611.

Smith, J., 2007. *Ireland's Magdalen laundries and the nation's architecture of containment.* Manchester: Manchester University Press.

Spirasi., 2019. *Spirasi - About.* [online] Available at: <http://spirasi.ie>.

Stonequist, E.V., 1937. *The Marginal Man: A study in personality and culture conflict.* New York: Russell & Russell

Thornton, L., 2014. *The Rights of Others: Asylum Seekers and Direct Provision in Ireland,'* *3*(2), pp.22-42.

Toar, M., O'Brien, K. K., & Fahey, T., 2009. Comparison of self-reported health & healthcare utilisation between asylum seekers and refugees: an observational study. *BMC Public Health*, 9(1), p.214.

University College Cork. 2021. *Irish Emigration History | University College Cork.* [online] Available at: <https://www.ucc.ie>.

United Nations, 2007. *Protecting Refugees & the Role of UNHCR.* United Nations.

Urban, E., 2012. The condition of female laundry workers in Ireland 1922-1996: A case of labour camps on trial. *Études Irlandaises*, *37*(2), pp.49-64.

Valiulis, M., 2011. The Politics of Gender in the Irish Free State, 1922–1937. *Women's History Review, 20*(4), pp.569-578.

Watts MJ, Bohle HG., 1993. The space of vulnerability: the causal structure of hunger and famine. *Progress in Human Geography, 17*, pp.43–67.

Whitebread, D., 2017. Free play and children's mental health. *The Lancet Child & Adolescent Health, 1*(3), pp.167-169.

Wilson, F. E., Hennessy, E., Dooley, B., Kelly, B. D., & Ryan, D. A., 2013. Trauma and PTSD rates in an Irish psychiatric population: a comparison of native and immigrant samples. *Disaster Health, 1*(2), pp.74-83.

Zizek, S., 2016. *Against the Double Blackmail: Refugees, Terror and Other Troubles with the Neighbours*. London: Penguin Random House.